Global
Communication

Global Communication

Is There a Place for Human Dignity?

Dafne Sabanes Plou

Risk
BOOK SERIES

WCC Publications, Geneva

Cover design: Rob Lucas
Back cover photo: Cristian Tauchner svd

ISBN 2-8254-1186-8

No. 71 in the Risk Book Series

Printed in Switzerland

Table of Contents

Introduction

A series of mergers involving media corporations worth thousands of millions of US dollars have demonstrated that information and communication have become expensive, profitable commodities, attracting more and more political and economic investment, and have underscored the close link between the global economic order and the production of information and communication. The free-market laws which govern the world economic order have strengthened the hold of big corporations in almost every sphere of the global telecommunications infrastructure, so that "the creation, production, control and distribution of media fare, *globally*, have increasingly become the private prerogative of a handful of rich multinational media corporations in the industrialized world".[1]

This development has amply confirmed the warnings about a concentration of resources and communication infrastructures issued in 1980 in the MacBride Report. Drafted by a committee appointed by UNESCO and chaired by the Irish Nobel and Lenin Peace Prize-winner Sean MacBride, *Many Voices, One World* offered a detailed analysis of growing transnational control over communications, and the disadvantages besetting the countries of the South in the exchange of information and communication technology. This domination not only covers written, radio and television communication, but also extends to transnational data banks and rights to artistic and intellectual property. Undergirding it is the role of intergovernmental bodies, so that, as Antonio Tujan Jr of the Philippines notes, "the World Trade Organization (WTO, formerly GATT) and the World Intellectual Property Organization (WIPO) play a decisive role in the economic and cultural relationship of countries. The General Agreement on Trade and Services (GATS) binds signatory countries to open their economies to 100-percent-equity foreign investments in such areas as media and communications, and prohibits the imposition of regulations limiting their operations. WIPO ensures the upgrading and improved enforcement of copyright laws protecting products and services of transnational communications corporations."[2]

The MacBride Report already expressed concern that the tendency to turn information into a commodity would set aside its role as a social good. Treating information as a commodity implies that knowledge is also a marketable good. The emergence of advanced technology has led to a redefinition of the manufacturing company as a laboratory in which ideas and knowledge are developed rather than simply a place of production. Dorith Grant-Wilson speaks of a "techno-paradigm shift" marked by the increasing importance of knowledge in the production of wealth:

> Accelerating scientific knowledge has increased in value as products and processes consist more of the power of the mind than of matter. This means that capital and technology are more focused on knowledge and service worker productivity, indicating the shift in importance from material capital and physical labour to intellectual capital and intellectual labour. [3]

Thus, copyright acquires considerable value in the global information economy. Instead of benefitting the public and the author or researcher or inventor, it has become an asset for the investor. The privatization of knowledge, scientific data and information enables transnational enterprises to acquire a monopoly over intellectual property for commercial purposes. The economic power of the corporations that control knowledge and technology ensures that this knowledge will never really be transferred to the purchasers. The latter are given the right to use the technology on lease for a given period of time, without ever gaining access to the knowledge itself. [4]

Largely under pressure from Western governments, led by the US, and communication corporations, the New World Information and Communication Order (NWICO) advocated by UNESCO and the non-aligned countries in the 1970s and 1980s came to be viewed as old-fashioned, even obsolete. It was said to be promoting government control over the media, and accused of curtailing freedom of the press. The non-aligned countries which fought so hard for a New International Economic Order which, together with the NWICO, would provide for a fair and equitable relationship between North and South, have lost clout in the post-cold war world. UNESCO itself heralded a major change of policy in 1987, when its new director general, Federico Mayor of Spain, declared to the press that UNESCO's "commitment is to defend the free flow of information".

UNESCO's medium-term plan for the 1990-95 period mentioned the NWICO only in the introduction and not in the operational sections of the document. In UNESCO's new strategy, "although there is some mention of concerns related to NWICO, such as cultural identity and endogenous media development, there is, on the other hand, virtually no mention of some of the most important issues linked to the NWICO, namely, transnational control of global media flows, the right to communicate, the rights and responsibilities of journalists, national communication policies, and the New International Economic Order."[5]

Alternative voices

Despite a powerful and well-orchestrated campaign against the NWICO, work in favour of this change continues to receive support from the Non-Aligned Movement and such non-governmental organizations (NGOs) as the International Association for Mass Communications Research (IAMCR), the World Association for Christian Communication (WACC) and the International Organization of Journalists (IOJ), as well as universities, scholars, journalists and communication experts. In 1989 these organizations created the MacBride Round Table, which meets every year in various parts of the world with experts from different countries who monitor global communication rights and balances, and report their findings and inquiries to community groups, UN agencies, NGOs and the media.

The Round Table has encouraged discussion of the themes of the MacBride Report, which continue to challenge us more than 15 years later. Its members are convinced that the right to communication must be defended as a fundamental human right, an individual as well as a social necessity. They are critical of the existing imbalance in the global flow of information and committed to dialogue and work in favour of greater equity in global communication, and in the flow of information within and between countries.

In their concern to achieve equity in the flow of information, to close the gap between the information-rich and the information-poor, members of the Round Table consider that people's participation is the key. This includes people's right to respond to what is communicated and to be involved in the decision-making processes. In this connection South-South cooperation can promote solidarity and confidence in the people's own ability to communicate. Different democratic and pluralistic structures are needed in order to "transcend the danger of both state and commercial media monopolization, and to ensure public control" (Prague statement, 1990). Such a transformation depends on a coalition of groups, social movements and organizations prepared to embark on this new struggle. "The democratization of communication should build on the strength of national coalitions entering into international cooperation on the basis of independence, equality and mutually beneficial objectives" (Istanbul statement, 1991).

The members of the MacBride Round Table are convinced that equity in the flow of information and communication "cannot lie with liberalized markets and deregulated and privatized industries, as the motive force and main instruments of change". On the contrary, "many observers are concerned that market forces, left unfettered, will significantly increase the gap between the haves and the have-nots" (Tunis statement, 1995).

According to the way the dominant economic system works, satisfying needs is a means of producing wealth. The notion of need has been replaced by that of demand. The media create needs to boost production and consumption, yielding greater profits. Satisfying real human requirements is not a priority; what the system is interested in is producing wealth. So long as precedence is given to economic over social development, the world's inhabitants will continue to be viewed as mere consumers.

For those who continue to work for a NWICO, people are the subjects of history and must be the centre of any proposal for development. This implies redefining the role of the community, civil society, the state and the market in building a communication model that respects people's dignity and ability to shape communication. It implies a search for strategies that build communities instead of markets.

NOTES

[1] From the conclusions of the group on economic issues at the second world congress of the World Association for Christian Communication (WACC), Metepec, Mexico, October 1994 (hereafter cited as Metepec).

[2] From his presentation to the workshop on economic issues in Metepec.

[3] Dorith Grant-Wisdom, "The Economics of Globalization: Implications for Communications and the Service Sector", in Hopeton S. Dunn, ed., *Globalization, Communications and Caribbean Identity*, Kingston, Jamaica, Ian Randle Publishers, 1995, p.5.

[4] Hopeton S. Dunn, "Policy Issues in Communication Technology Use", in *ibid.*, p.21.

[5] Hamid Mowlana and Colleen Roach, "New Information and Communication Order: Overview of Recent Developments and Activities", in Michael Traber and Kaarle Nordenstreng, eds, *Few Voices, Many Worlds*, London, WACC, 1992, p.7.

1. The Media Set the Agenda

What does it mean to live in a world in which information and communication have become global? The neo-liberal market laws governing political and economic decisions in the North, exported to and imposed on many countries in the South, specify that it is necessary to standardize not only production but also consumer tastes in order to sell more and increase profits. Nearly 10 percent of the world's economy is currently based on information and communication, and it is forecast that, in the next century, communication and information will be the largest industry in the world. The race between big information and communication corporations to corner ever-larger segments of the world market springs from the need to control even the most remote markets in order to sell their products.

Illustrating the rapid growth and concentration of the communication industry is the difficulty today of finding a Western company that deals only in newspapers. In general, what were once newspaper companies are now large multimedia empires, producing books and magazines, controlling AM and FM radio, antenna and cable television and, in some cases, film-making as well. The 1994 merger of Disney and Time-Warner demonstrates the many possibilities for vertiginous growth and concentration in this field.

And the effects? In many countries you can buy a newspaper, listen to the radio and watch a television programme produced by a single private multimedia company and receive the same information, the same opinion, the same analysis. Does this make our societies more democratic? Despite the illusion of being better informed, are people not increasingly being limited to what the interests of a private group are prepared to let them know?

One of the key questions at this juncture relates to possibilities of equitable access to all this information and communication. Statistics show that 90 percent of the global telecommunications network serves only 15 percent of the world. Howard Frederick painted a dramatic picture of this situation at a 1993 forum of Latin American communicators:

— 95 percent of all computers are in the developed countries;
— the remaining countries contain three-quarters of the world's population, but produce only 30 percent of the world's newspapers;
— approximately 75 percent of the world suffers from a shortage of books, and a New York reader consumes more paper each Sunday than an African in a year;
— only 17 countries have a gross national product greater than total expenditure on advertising in the USA;
— four news agencies control 96 percent of the entire flow of news in the world. [1]

The tremendous gap between the infomation-rich and the information-poor, so clearly highlighted in the 1980 MacBride Report, is widening; it reflects unfair, unequal relations between countries. In the North and among a few expert groups in the South, communication via Internet is growing in importance, and the possibilities for participating in global discussion forums and taking economic, financial, military and public policy decisions in cyberspace are increasing. But in many other countries it is virtually impossible to obtain a telephone line, the indispensable tool for computer communication and the operation of the new integrated telecommunications system. This gap is not accidental. One hundred years after the telephone was invented, a large portion of the world's population does not have one. In 1992 fifty countries, inhabited by over half the world's population, had only one telephone line per 100 inhabitants. Seventy-one percent of the telephone lines in the world are in high-income countries, while low-income ones own 4 percent.

The MacBride Round Table meeting in Tunisia in 1995 looked at the African situation in light of the creation of the "information superhighway". African communicators realize that their continent not only lacks access to the telephone, but seems "to have lost its strategic significance for the West since the end of the superpower rivalry" (Tunis statement). They fear that the much-vaunted superhighway will go down the coast of the continent, missing out 70 percent of Africa's population. For this population, without electricity or access to a phone, there is little prospect of major changes in the future either. The inhabitants of the innumerable villages in the African interior have so little purchasing power that big information corporations do not even take them into account in their plans. Those who do not consume in accordance with market expectations are excluded from the consumer goods and services market, the labour and education market. They do not come within the scope of the "equal opportunities" vaunted by supposedly democratic societies.

This policy of exclusion, where the decision-making power of a country with little clout as a producer or consumer is curtailed in international forums by advancing monopolies and the steamroller effect of market policies, demonstrates that today it is the private corporation that is most capable of coping with the economic and social transformations of this post-industrial era. The inequality and exclusion prevailing at the international level are also reflected within the countries of the South, whose economies have had to adjust rapidly to the demands of neo-liberalism.

The consequences of these policies for a typical Latin American country, according to researcher José Martinez Terrero, are that "the entire country revolves around private enterprise — a diminished state, a frightened people, nervous armed forces, badly-paid teachers, a moribund health system, a worried church, hungry unemployed, indigenous communities subject to discrimination... The whole of civil society is dislocated, shattered, disorganized, not knowing how to proceed. Private enterprise is the best organized sector."[2] And, moving ahead of society and governments, it is able to impose decisions without regard to the consequences.

These have not been long in coming. Economic analysts consider that the 1980s were a "lost decade" for Latin America. While many countries re-established democratic systems after repressive military dictatorships, the economic situation deteriorated, as did people's standard of living —

not because people ceased to work and produce, but because all their efforts were channelled into paying the foreign debt, neglecting investment in education, health, housing, better wages and job creation. The only ones to benefit from this policy were the banks and multinational corporations. The economies of the developing world, which transferred an average of US\$25,000 million a year to the industrialized countries, were drained dry. The fact that 14 million children under the age of five die each year from the combined effect of malnutrition and preventable and curable diseases is perhaps the most painful reminder of how decisions taken on a macro-economic level fail to take account of human realities.

Under such circumstances how can those who really believe in communication that does not impose patterns of behaviour and consumption, but allows for free creativity and plurality of symbols, images and statements — communication that is inspired by solidarity, commitment to those who have the least and democratic participation — respond?[3] Will it be possible to replace "globalization from above" by "globalization from below"? For Dutch researcher Cees Hamelink, the use of the information superhighway creates serious ambiguities in this respect.[4] He considers that this highway will be the biggest supermarket in the world, that it will include all the telecommunications, computer, radio and television transmission networks and that it will meet the needs of the global economy by preaching the "fundamentalist gospel" of neo-liberalism, thereby ensuring that the only regulator of global trade relations is the market.

The creation and development of the information superhighway has the strong political support of governments in the US and the European Union. The US vice-president Al Gore, for example, has presented the superhighway project as contributing to sustainable development: if people can communicate with each other, they will be able to solve their economic and ecological problems and improve their health and education. But we must not be naive, Hamelink warns. If, as Gore's description would have it, the superhighway will usher in a "new era of Athenian democracy", we must remember that the majority of the population of Athens were not considered "citizens" — women, slaves, children, the freed, foreigners — and were thus excluded.

When leaders from the Group of Seven industrialized countries (G-7) discussed this issue in 1995, they agreed that two fundamental principles — liberalization and universal service (access for all) — should govern its functioning. However, it is well known that their real commitment is to the first point, which is where powerful corporations will act and invest. Universal access will have to be defended. Who will be responsible for ensuring that no one is excluded or discriminated against, thereby respecting the right to communication of all the inhabitants of this world?

Guatemalan poet Julia Esquivel nevertheless believes it is important to fight for "globalization from below", even within the Internet. [5] "Real communication develops from the base," she says, and even cyberspace can be open to participation, the sharing of ideas, the struggle for human dignity wherever it is threatened. "Real communication must wage a cultural battle to dislodge miscommunication. Real communication loves life and rejects contamination born of false power. If communication is understood to mean dialogue, human encounter and understanding, it can be given to others like bread, food, an incarnate word offered by women in solidarity with other women, and men in solidarity with other men. Jesus offers himself in the bread and the wine, and tells us that the whole of life can be food for others."

Many of those active in the quest for justice, peace and the integrity of creation also believe that the advanced tools created for military, financial or commercial purposes can be harnessed to spread their message and organized in order to make "globalization from below" a reality, thereby limiting the power exercised by just a few corporate interests.

Consensus, awareness and manipulation

Different theories can guide critical analysis of the messages conveyed by the mass media. The work done by various Latin American study centres over the past few decades emphasizes the attitude of those receiving the messages, the way they interact with the media and the manner in which media and society become dependent on each other.

The British model of cultural studies developed by Stuart Hall has made an important contribution to research on active reception as it seeks to discover the meaning of media messages for each group or social class. Media content, on the whole, tends to further the ideology of the dominant class, but messages end up being decoded and understood in relation to an audience's social status. A key insight of this approach is to see the audience as participating in the message reception process, negotiating and even resisting media content.

Peruvian researcher Rosa Maria Alfaro points out that, among schools of thought that strongly criticize the media, the European school "demonizes the media in accordance with a long-standing tradition critical of the culture industry but, in turn, exaggerates the media's ability to manipulate", whereas a different school of thought, prominent in the US, "with a more optimistic vision of the media, expects democratizing effects on behaviour". [6]

In both interpretations the media are deemed to be "tools with an enormous capacity to influence people's thoughts and feelings in a linear, mechanical way, either destroying them like a deadly weapon, or saving them like a healing magic potion... The links between media and society, communication and global cultural dynamics, production and consumption as part of people's daily lives are not sufficiently examined... Power is conceived as something separate from people and social organization itself." [7]

Are those receiving the messages so easy to manipulate, so meek and passive, so incapable of selecting? It might be interesting to compare how, in societies where there is greater awareness of gender, the media steer clear of sexist advertisements, respect a balance between men and women in their radio and television programmes and carefully avoid stereotyped jokes. The same is true of certain large corporations which have opted to produce advertisements depicting people of different races doing things together. The media seek the approval of the audience, and they know when it is receptive to this kind of non-discriminatory image or message.

To go a step further, we can say that there is complicity, mutual satisfaction and convergence between those who transmit and those who receive the messages, although this relationship is unequal because it is the media that set the tone. Even so, the receivers select, relate what they experience with what they see, ask and get answers, build consensus, make value judgments, and also offer dissent and spontaneous resistance. People are not passive. Rather, there is always an active relationship with the media, so that "words, attitudes and images acquire meaning, in that everyone talks and listens to one another, even through silence". [8]

We live in a mass culture; we can say that we have already moved from the "global village" to the "global city". Mass culture exists and is a part of us, who also build it. Latin American intellectuals like Nestor Garcia Canclini describe "hybrid cultures" born of cultural intermingling; the result is a reorganization of the symbols market. Reggae music, for example, is highly popular in Argentina and Uruguay where there are virtually no traces of black culture. High school students protest against a superficial consumer society by listening to Bob Marley's "freedom songs". Latin American "soap operas", produced for audiences familiar with relations between social classes on that continent, touch television audiences in Africa who can identify with the plots even if they do not understand the Spanish dialogue. A friend from Nairobi told me that her mother never missed an episode of "The Rich Also Cry", whose multi-millionairess heroine cannot find her only son, whom she gave to an orphanage twenty years earlier when she was a poor, lost waif. When I asked her what attracted Kenyans to this very

Latin American melodrama, she answered simply: "It is because they talk about human relations, feelings, hopes. They are different from 'Dallas' or 'Dynasty', where the characters vie with each other for money and power. The Latin American soap operas are closer to us because they show ordinary people; they show that family ties and love stories still mean a lot in people's lives." Maybe soap operas are an unsuspected avenue of South-South communication!

Rolando Pérez Vela from Peru thinks mass media culture has helped indigenous communities gain access to modernity. "In Latin America, the door to modernity is the audio-visual media and not books. Largely illiterate or semi-literate peasants, Indians and workers have joined the modern world thanks to the electronic media. One of the first things the Indian communities displaced by the war against the Shining Path decided was to install their own dish antenna once they returned home. They do not want to go on living in isolation in the mountains. They want to be in contact with the world, because they want to feel part of it."[9]

Something similar is happening in the poor neighbourhoods of Guatemala City, where people who live in the poorest houses have cable TV, despite their meagre income. Alfaro points out in her study that "the globalization of the economy, politics and cultural production has led the grass-roots to view themselves as citizens of the world, though they are not yet treated as citizens of their own country."[10]

Based on a theory that links viewers' social and psychological status and their televiewing behaviour, Antonio Carlos Ruotolo of the Methodist Higher Institute of Sao Bernardo do Campo, Brazil, conducted a survey in 1992 on television-viewing in a district of Sao Paulo with a population of nearly ten million.[11] The survey identified five types of television viewers: (1) Some people watch television to keep abreast of what is happening in their city, country or in the world. This group, for whom watching television is a "pastime", account for 24 percent of the audience studied. (2) A similar 24 percent watch television in order to seek information that allows them to form opinions and compare these with others. They feel involved in events and enjoy discussing what they have seen on television. They do not watch TV for pleasure, entertainment or as a pastime. These are the viewers who are most concerned by social problems, but are least convinced that the economic crisis is the country's main problem. (3) A third type of viewer also wishes to be well informed, but this is linked to the desire to be respected by others for one's knowledge of events. The information these people (11 percent of those surveyed) gather from television helps them to interact socially and achieve recognition. (4) For 18 percent of viewers, television is company, a form of entertainment and relaxation that enables them to forget their worries. They are not interested in getting information. Of the five groups these people watch television the most. (5) A fifth category, constituting 23 percent of viewers, has a varied and active relationship with the television. These people seek information topics useful in their daily lives. They view television as a source of entertainment, a pastime that helps them to relax, to experience emotion as they share in events and to dream.

Feelings, emotions and also ideas are involved in the interaction between media and audience. "The media both transmit and add to social complexity. They are important, if complex, factors in the development and reproduction of culture, forums where consensus and dissent take shape. They are installed within social systems... They do not invent evil but rework it; they are not the only causes but, in any case, share and organize the damage wreaked by society itself."[12] Audiences are not always easy to manipulate, although there is some danger of manipulation. "While there is empathy and complicity, it is not a linear relationship in which everyone understands, interprets and uses the message in the same way. The media are not merely tools of manipulation; people do not passively, naïvely believe everything they hear and see. Social experience also constitutes a symbolic capital that challenges what comes over the media."[13]

Jamaica's population of just over 2.3 million (1991 census) owns an estimated 700,000 television sets and over 1.8 million radios. One recent study on Jamaican youth revealed a "love of American music among upper- and middle-class youth, and their disdain for local traditions, dances and reggae music". [14] This was identified as evidence of cultural dependency. "The sentiment that what is local is inferior is still quite prevalent, and status is conferred by the extent to which one adopts North American fashion and technology, and the frequency of travel to the US." The media in Jamaica and the rest of the Caribbean have a history of foreign ownership dating to the days of colonialism.

Uruguayan writer Eduardo Galeano has described his great surprise at seeing Cuna Indian children on the San Blas archipelago in Panama acting out the myths of the American Far West in their games. They were playing cowboys and Indians; what made it worse was that none of the Cuna children wanted to "play Indian". Galeano sees this as clear proof that the cultural industry controls society on a planetary scale, and holds up "a deceitful mirror that teaches Latin American children to look at themselves with the same eyes that despise them, and makes them docilely accept as their destiny the reality that humiliates them". [15]

Why do young people and children adopt the model of the oppressor? The underlying desire is apparently not to be identified with the losers — in this case, the colonized. The easy way out is to stop resisting and adopt the garb of the oppressor. It is hard to resist, for resistance often means isolation, at least temporarily.

Galeano argues that the major challenge facing com-municators is to re-create and recover alternative myths. "The myths of the culture of humiliation are not the only possible myths. There are myths born of the history of peoples, cultures, traditions linked to the land, that are myths of liberation... We must work to recover our collective memory, which appears to be struck by amnesia."

Sometimes the oppressed have publicized their own interpretation of history. The use of the media by the indigenous peoples of Latin America on the 500th anniversary of the European conquest of America is a case in point. Their patient litany condemning triumphalistic celebrations of the conquest successfully destroyed any festive plans. Official acts of commemoration were forced to take account of the 500 years of oppression of the original peoples, and no government, let alone the Spanish crown, dared to celebrate Christopher Columbus's arrival in America.

The campaign waged by the American indigenous peoples received worldwide support, and won the Nobel Peace Prize for Rigoberta Menchu, a Guatemalan Indian whose family fell victim to state terrorism. Thanks to this campaign the UN designated 1993 as the "International Year of Indigenous Peoples". From the depths of silence, those who had been hushed for so many centuries exercised their right to be the subjects of communication, to build their dignity. They not only awoke a large portion of white Latin American society to the real situation, but also gained its backing. As pointed out by Bishop Samuel Ruiz of Chiapas, in Mexico, "we have to listen to the victims' version because total non-communication can become a force of communication." [16]

Messages conveyed by the mass media can trigger hidden motivations, old resentments, unspoken prejudices, hatred buried in the deepest recesses of a person's being or frustrated desires latent in society. These can be reactivated by clever and persistent campaigns.

From the moment the Pentagon began to prepare for the Gulf War, US television devoted 2855 minutes to the war effort, and only 29 minutes to information about opposition to it. Was this imbalance to feed a latent desire for triumph and glory among the American people? Was it to achieve a consensus in favour of a military escalation in which the enemy was practically invisible, and no one knew exactly how many people died, nor what damage was caused to the surviving population and the environment? This was a case of censorship with a television camera in hand. Militarism needed a popular consensus to implement its plans.

The Gulf War was an unprecendented communications event. Censorship was applied on a global scale. But was it applied from above, or did public opinion itself shy away from information? In his analysis Costa Rican social researcher Franz J. Hinkelammert maintains that public opinion *wanted* to be protected against information it did not want to hear. "Amnesia about Iraq was created on purpose. Public opinion itself produced it. There was never any news except in the *samizdat* of marginal cultures, considered subversive. Public opinion, to which information is addressed, refused to be informed. The fact it knew virtually nothing shows, however, that it knew everything, but not in the form of specific news. As it knew all, albeit not in the form of information, public opinion could act as though it knew nothing. The fact that it insisted on censorship proves it knew a huge genocide was being carried out there... This censorship is thus 'democratic' in that it was requested by the vast majority of the population." [17]

In analyzing what fostered the ethnic hatred leading to the massacre that left between 500,000 and a million people dead in Rwanda in 1994, all the reports point out the role of Radio Television Libre Mille Collines (RTLM), a private station which began an intensive hate campaign against the Tutsis in the autumn of 1993. RTLM encouraged "racist propaganda that was the result of a political policy elaborated and applied systematically from the 1920s onwards in the media, political thought and official documents... Discrimination was not excluded by post-colonial governments, but rather they grafted other techniques, such as the so-called policy of ethnic and regional balance, onto it. In addition, organized massacres were presented as inter-ethnic cleansing." [18]

Hugh McCullum, a Canadian journalist living in Nairobi who visited Rwanda numerous times during the war, points out that the use of modern propaganda methods was "frighteningly reminiscent of the extremely successful 'big lie' philosophy of Josef Goebbels in the 1930s and 1940s". [19] Not only was RTLM not taken off the air, says McCullum, but to his knowledge, no Rwandan church leader ever spoke out against the station and some indeed broadcast "moments of meditation" over it.

"Radio is normally regarded in Rwanda as the voice of authority, a view that arises directly from a society in which the oral tradition is very strong," says Frances D'Souza, director of Article 19, a London-based research and information centre on censorship. "The murderous and well-timed broadcasts in the local language were imposed on an illiterate, landless, unemployed and poverty-stricken nation, who were constantly told that their problems were caused by Tutsis, and that by eliminating the Tutsis they could reclaim their dignity and their land."[20]

Many parallels regarding the use of the media to encourage war can be seen in the former Yugoslavia, where television was the predominant medium. D'Souza reports that "the government-controlled media constantly put before the people words and images of crude nationalism that played upon ancient fears existing long before the setting up of the Federal Republic of Yugoslavia". Journalists "either agreed to support government misinformation, distortion and propaganda, or were co-opted to do so. Those who refused were instantly dismissed, threatened and some even murdered." Vicious ethnic jokes, especially against the *mullahs* in Bosnia, were broadcast. Criminal murders were presented as ethnically-motivated killings. "The language of war and ethnic hatred became increasingly commonplace," affirms D'Souza. Thus objectivity became impossible. "The media in all three republics cashed in on this division, and exacerbated it to the point of, and beyond, genocide."

The ancestral hatreds in both these cases were not created but rekindled by the media. But if the foundations for war and racial hatred were already in place, the structures of such extreme cruelty, terror and injustice could not have been built without the systematic use of electronic media to bolster perverse and untruthful discourse. In Rwanda RTLM attracted a large audience of young people by playing music from Zaire, the Congo and

Cameroon, as well as reggae. It recruited capable, popular professionals from both intellectual circles and the lower and peasant classes. In former Yugoslavia, death threats were used to ensure that few opposed the rules of the game defined for the media. Frances D'Souza concludes that "governments need their citizens not only to support the war, but to fight it for them. The media are needed to reinforce the intention and policies of government at every turn."

How can the spiral of lies and violence be halted? How can the media be prevented from falling in with policies of this kind? For Rwandan journalist Tharcisse Gatwa "the practice of journalism rests on a fundamental principle: telling the truth. Important characteristics of truth-telling are honesty, perception, integrity and professionalism... Rewriting any news that could cost lives, and the elimination of deliberate bias are of paramount importance. The option for humane journalism seems to me the best instrument for a profession that is part of humanity."[21]

To contend with the power of the media and the information we receive as a result of decisions made by others, Cees Hamelink says it is important for people to understand that they must start asserting their power to reject the barrage of unwanted information and promotion of unnecessary goods. "Together we can say: the rubbish being thrown at us is not what we need. Or the lies and propaganda either. It is good to worry about the physical environment, but we must also be concerned with our information and cultural environment. Both are part of our future. We must stop silently accepting trashy, deceitful messages. We have more power than we think. As the media's receivers, can we create alliances? Can we negotiate? We have enormous potential and must prepare to use it."[22]

"The powers-that-be," adds Galeano, "want us to accept reality instead of challenging it, to resign ourselves to the future, instead of imagining it. God loves those who want to live — to live with dignity."[23]

Ecumenical responses to globalization

The London-based World Association for Christian Communication (WACC) has followed the international discussions on the NWICO step by step and offered a forum in which church-related and Christian communicators in particular can debate new policies based on the MacBride Report. Organizations of Roman Catholic communicators — OCIC (cinema and audiovisual media), UNDA (radio and television) and UCIP (press) — have also been involved in this debate, and remain critical of the progressive globalization of communication as a result of the development of electronic media. Participants in the WACC's second world congress in Metepec, Mexico, in October 1995 warned against trying to avoid this issue: "Communication is threatened once again by the development of new and expensive tools that deepen the division between rich and poor, even within richer nations. This is serious, because the tools of modern communication set the tone, the values and the norms of modern society. Withdrawal from new technological development to a reaffirmation of personal people-to-people communication is illusionary; modern communication is the fabric, not just a facet, of modern society. Young people especially, whether rich or poor, will 'want it'."[24]

During the World Council of Churches' sixth assembly in Vancouver, Canada, in 1983, one group of participants worked for an entire week on the issue of "Communicating Credibly". While the NWICO was not specifically on its agenda, the group acknowledged the progress of mass communication techniques. It warned against the growth and unequal distribution of the media, and pointed out that "we find ourselves in a situation in which a few claim to speak in the name of all and to all, at both the national and the international level. Too often, the mass media serve solely to confirm that injustice. Most ordinary men and women are excluded except as objects of the media."[25]

The assembly called on the churches to relate to the media in three ways — pastorally, evangelically and prophetically. "Pastorally, it must try to understand the tensions of those who work in the media and assist them to perform their work in ways which affirm human values. Evangelically, the church must resist the temptation to use the media in ways which violate people's dignity and manipulate them, but rather should proclaim with humility and conviction the truth entrusted to it." And in its prophetic role "it must provide a continuing critique of the performance, content and techniques of the mass media and the ideologies which lie behind them".

The Manila Declaration, approved by 450 Christian communicators from 80 countries attending WACC's first world congress, recognized that "communication is a crucial issue... for the future of humankind. It can lead to reconciliation or destruction. It can bring knowledge, truth and inspiration, or withhold knowledge and spread disinformation and lies."[26] The Manila Declaration insists that communication must be in the service of society and humanity, and that it is everyone's responsibility — governments and formal and informal social organizations — to ensure that neither society nor humanity is manipulated or unduly appropriated by a single power centre.

The Manila congress theme, "Communication for Community", emphasized the need to build democratic communication based on people's power to increase their freedom to communicate, and communicate among themselves. Part of its appeal to Christian communicators to revolutionize values and social priorities focused on overcoming militaristic, violent, discriminatory, sexist and consumption-oriented language. Noting that we live in two inter-connected spheres — the natural environment and the environment created by human beings, which includes culture and receives its energy from the community — it argued that the call to "protect the environment" implies challenging anything that has poisoned either of these.

The Manila Declaration also highlighted the concentration and power of media which treat their audiences as objects destined to consume what is offered them, rather than as subjects of communication. It appealed to the churches to democratize their own media, and rebuked communication professionals who neglect the struggle of people's movements for freedom and justice. It supported journalists, communicators and cultural workers whose defence of the right to communication threatens them with job losses, persecution and even assassination.

Participants at the Manila congress prepared to continue questioning the commercial and ideological power that corporations wield through the media. "We feel privileged to work towards a new communication environment which challenges unjust power structures," they said. "Christian communicators have no other option but to throw their lot in with the poor, oppressed and marginalized who bear the hallmark of God's communication."

The Manila meeting had a decisive impact on another consultation organized by WACC and IPAL (Institute for Latin America) in November 1990. Christian and lay communicators from across the continent gathered in Lima, Peru, to analyze what had occurred in world communication in the ten years since the MacBride Report. A "Lima Declaration" expressed concern at the "increasing homogenization of universal tastes at the lowest levels" and the "silencing of more and more people by cutting off their sources, creativity and audio-visual media, or by expropriating their telecommunications infrastructure". [27] A "new order" of communication is being imposed, the Declaration observed, but it is quite different from what was envisaged by the NWICO: "Its unique, excluding and exclusive logic is that of economic returns, ratings, advertising and one-way direction of global communication relationships between human beings."

Latin American communicators at the Lima meeting pledged to work "for full and effective democratization of the capacity to create, send and receive messages, and... legislation which guarantees satisfactory levels of pluralism and participation in communication; for real and objective freedom for all means of sending and receiving information; for the freedom to seek different solutions to different international, national or group problems of communication; for change in societies which are basically receivers and dependents into societies which produce news, messages and programmes, without which minimum standards of balance, reciprocity or integration will never be achieved." They also pledged "to promote by the most imaginative and practical means the indigenous production of news, messages and programmes, as well as their use, exhibition and distribution; to struggle for the just and self-evident goal of establishing real public communication services; and to stimulate broader and better communication services, promoting in particular participation by women and ensuring, as well, the presence of every sector of society including religious, political, ethnic and other minorities."

When the World Council of Churches' seventh assembly met in Canberra, Australia, in 1991, it was against the background of a particularly vivid demonstration of the economic and ideological power exercised through globalized communications: the coverage of the Gulf War, especially by major transnational television channels like CNN, to which we referred earlier.

Communication and its challenge for Christians and ecumenism were taken up in Canberra under the theme "Spirit of Truth — Set Us Free", in which one sub-group discussed "The challenge of communication for liberation". [28] The group recommended that "churches should monitor the role of the communication media, and vigorously object when what is communicated distorts the truth, reinforces stereotypes or sanctions violent behaviour". Only when we are informed fairly about a situation "can we be free to respond to our brothers and sisters in need... We must find ways to guarantee that our member churches have access to non-censored information so that we can act... We need to communicate the cause of justice, peace and the integrity of creation."

The Canberra assembly reaffirmed what was said at Vancouver in 1983: that communication is prophetic and that, in the light of the Spirit, it "supports and sustains the building of a community of justice and equips us to challenge the powers that are opposed to the Spirit of truth". It criticized the "governments of Northern democracies" which "control what the media can communicate. The truth is not told and we cannot exercise our free judgment." It also criticized the control of audiovisual production by the dominant culture and asked whether communication technologies should not "give a voice to the voiceless".

It appealed to the WCC to support the NWICO and urged the churches to enable the powerless to express their demands in their own way; to speak out prophetically for the rights of the powerless; to organize boycotts of any products sold by those who sponsor violent, sexist, racist, pornographic or obscene programmes; and to promote media-awareness training at all levels.

From the Roman Catholic side, a 1992 Pastoral Instruction from the Pontifical Council for Social Communications analyzed the globalization of communications as the background to guidelines for pastoral work in this field. *Aetatis Novae* points out that "today much that men and women know and think about life is conditioned by the media; to a considerable extent human experience itself is an experience of media." It recognizes that "the power of the media extends to defining not only what people will think but even what they will think about. Reality, for many, is what the media recognize as real; what the media do not acknowledge seems of little importance." In this sense, "de facto silence can be imposed on individuals or groups whom the media ignore; and even the voice of the gospel can be muted, though not entirely stilled, in this way. It is important, therefore, that Christians find ways to furnish the missing information to those deprived of it, and also to give a voice to the voiceless." [29]

For the Pontifical Council the social communication media should serve people and cultures, dialogue, human community and social progress, ecclesial communion and a new evangelization. It strongly defends the right of all to communication, calling it unacceptable "that freedom of communication should depend upon wealth, education or political power". In the defence of human cultures, "grass-roots and traditional media not only provide an important forum for local cultural expression, but develop competence for active participation in shaping and using mass media... In all cases people ought to be able to participate actively, autonomously and responsibly in the processes of communication which, in so many ways, help to shape the conditions of their lives."

The Vatican document also underscores the link between communication and peoples' development: "accessible point-to-point communication and mass media offer many people a more adequate opportunity to participate in the modern world economy, to experience freedom of expression and to contribute to the emergence of peace and justice in the world."

An inter-regional meeting of Christian theologians and communicators in Quezon City, Philippines, in 1992 provided an interesting exchange of insights on the globalization of communications. Organized by Intermedia, an agency of the National Council of Churches in the USA (NCCCUSA), and WACC-Asia, and co-sponsored by the Christian Conference of Asia (CCA), the Asian Social Institute, People in Communication and the National Council of Churches in the Philippines (NCCP), the meeting centred on the theme "Global Communication and Justice".

Asian participants spoke of the ongoing colonization of Asia in a situation where "the purveyors of domination have managed to link with transnational corporations engaged in the media business. Control over the minds and the existence of the people has been magnified with the influx of programmes and technology produced in the North and broadcast in the South."[30] Moreover, they suggested, the church in Asia has been an ally of foreign domination, and has failed in its proclamation of the gospel out of an inability to understand the suffering caused by colonization or to identify with the culture of its people. Nor has it understood the power that communication could lend to its missionary task.

However, they added, this is changing, and the church "has come to realize the big role it can play in the unshackling of Asia's bondage to the West... The awakening of the church in Asia needs to be sustained. It needs to maintain the dialogue between the culture of the church and the culture of the people. It needs to understand more deeply the issues that confront the peoples of Asia. And it needs to rediscover the latent power of media in preaching the good news of justice, freedom and peace."

The North American participants also issued a declaration, which expressed concern about exported communication that ignores local cultures and social questions and imposes market policies and mass media culture with hegemonistic tendencies. They recognized that "if we are to achieve a true sense of global awareness and commitment, Americans must come to understand and recognize the importance of all people's stories. Asia has been exposed to American stories through our media for decades. We must now begin to be exposed to the stories of Asia and other continents."[31]

North American participants pledged to work to get churches "to adopt the issue of solidarity and participation with victims of cultural domination as a primary mission priority" and "include communication in all peace, justice, and advocacy agendas". They acknowledged that examining relations with other cultures within their own country is also integral to the search for more just global communication. "The churches must work to strengthen the voices of those in North America who are marginalized by the dominant culture."

In mid-1992 the NCCCUSA and the North American Region of WACC sponsored a second consultation on "Global Communications for Justice and Peace", this time in New York. Its aim was to offer people responsible for communication in member churches an opportunity to draw on their own working experience to make concrete recommendations to their churches.

Participants voiced concern that new technologies and mass media have taken away people's control over their own communication — the heart of cultural and economic life — and that "the media shape our consciousness and our quest for the meaning of life". Given this context, they saw the churches as "a global communication system through which the voices of those rendered voiceless because they lack access to the media can be raised to question these trends... Churches are committed to development through empowerment, and empowerment through communication."[32]

They agreed on the need "to strengthen the voices of the oppressed persons in North America and around the world who are marginalized by dominant culture," and said they would work to advocate for their participation in both mass and in alternative media, and "to affirm the right and necessity for all people, individually and collectively, to develop their own particular style and forms of message content, advertising, information and entertainment, and to protect themselves from the monopoly of external interests".

The essential message running through all of the meetings on global communication which we have surveyed here is that the right to communicate is essential for human dignity and for building a fair, democratic society, and that it is up to Christians and the churches to ensure these rights are fully enjoyed in the "global city" in which we live.

NOTES

[1] Howard Frederick, "Communication in Contemporary Society", in *Breaking the Silence*, Report of the Latin American Encounter on Alternative and Popular Communication Media, Quito, Latin American Information Agency, 1993, p.42.

[2] José Martinez Terrero, "Current Challenges of Alternative and Popular Communication", in *ibid.*, p.54.

[3] Cf. Hopeton Dunn's keynote address in Metepec: "Communication for Human Dignity: Empowering the Voiceless in an Era of Globalization".

[4] Cees Hamelink, presentation at Metepec on "Globalization and Human Dignity" (on tape).

5 Julia Esquivel, presentation in the panel at Metepec on "Latin America: from reflection to action".

6 Rosa Maria Alfaro, *Communication for Another Development*, Lima, "Calandria" Association of Social Communicators, 1993, p.23.

7 *Ibid.*, p.20.

8 *Ibid.*, p.28.

9 Rolando Pérez Vela, interviewed in Metepec.

10 Rosa Maria Alfaro, "From Popular Cultures to Political Transformations", in *Entre Publicos y Ciudadanos*, Lima, "Calandria" Association of Social Communicators, 1994, p.89.

11 Antonio Ruotolo, "Typology of Television Viewers in Sao Paulo ABC", in *TV for Whom?*, notebook with the findings of the symposium on this topic sponsored by WACC-Latin America, Sao Paulo, Dec. 1992.

12 Rosa Maria Alfaro, "Heavy Policies for Light Media", *op. cit.*, p.130.

13 *Ibid.*

14 Hilary Brown, "American Media Impact on Jamaican Youth", in *Globalization, Communications and Caribbean Identity*, p.60.

15 Eduardo Galeano, "Notes on the Media of Incommunication", Metepec.

16 Samuel Ruiz, lecture at Metepec (on tape).

17 Franz J. Hinkelammert, *Culture of Hope and Society without Exclusion*, San José, Costa Rica, DEI, 1995, p.47.

18 Tharcisse Gatwa, "Ethnic Conflict and the Media: The Case of Rwanda", *Media and Development*, Vol. 42, no. 3, 1995, p.18.

19 Hugh McCullum, *The Angels Have Left Us: the Rwanda Tragedy and the Churches*, Geneva, WCC, 1995.

20 Frances D'Souza, lecture on "Communication and Peace" at Metepec.

21 Tharcisse Gatwa, *loc. cit.*

22 Cees Hamelink, *loc. cit.*

23 Eduardo Galeano, *loc. cit.*

24 Conclusions of the issue group on "Christian Communication" in Metepec.

25 "Communicating Credibly", in David Gill, ed., *Gathered for Life*, official report of the WCC's sixth assembly, Geneva, WCC, 1983, pp.103-10.

26 *Communication for Community: The Manila Declaration*, London, WACC, 1989.

27 *"Towards a New Communication: The Lima Declaration*, London, WACC, 1990.

24

28 "The Challenge of Communication for Liberation", in Michael Kinnamon, ed., *Signs of the Spirit*, official report of the WCC's seventh assembly, Geneva, WCC, 1991, pp.83-85.
29 *Aetatis Novae*, Pontifical Council for Social Communications, Vatican City, Libreria Editrice Vaticana, 1992.
30 Statement of Asian participants in the consultation report, *Global Communication and Justice*, Quezon City, Intermedia and WACC-Asian Region, 1992.
31 "North American Findings of the Manila Consultation", *ibid*.
32 "Global Communications for Justice and Peace", policy statement of the NCCCUSA, New York, 1992.

2. The Search for Democracy

In a newspaper article at the beginning of 1996, the Peruvian-Spanish writer Mario Vargas Llosa, a well-known advocate of neo-liberal economic, social and cultural policies, asserted that the monotony and superficiality of current television programming is due to lack of competition. The answer, he said, is to open up media frontiers to the information, entertainment and fiction superhighways. [1] Yet in countries where open competition is already the rule, and people can tune in to dozens of different television channels, the programming on offer does not evidence much variety. Viewers "zap" from channel to channel in growing despair at finding only more of the same. Radio too offers the same diet of commercial music, commentaries on the same events from similar standpoints, undifferentiated analysis of information. The media belong to big communications corporations whose main aim is profit, and programme content is dictated by commercial ends.

Is free commercial competition the only way to improve television programmes? Are we not entitled to see other events and images, to hear voices, facts and opinions whose choice is not determined by commercial considerations? We must be aware of the ambiguity in the term "free flow of information and communication". When corporations call for this, it is because they want to expand their business and gain a greater share of the market. When civil society calls for this, it has in mind the right to communicate as a social good, the right of its members to be informed, express themselves, meet together and organize to protect common interests and to build just and equitable relations.

The MacBride Report devotes an entire chapter to the democratization of communication. [2] It sees the right to communicate as the foundation of a free, just and egalitarian society. This includes the right to inform and be informed, the right to privacy and participation in public communication, the right of citizens to participate in decision-making by contributing their opinions, ideas and suggestions, without discrimination, conditions or control. Both public and private media must be subject to these requirements.

It should be noted that, in general, the battle between the public and private sectors for ownership of the media leaves out a whole range of ownership possibilities. Neither governments, who often use the public media as a mouthpiece for their own interests and authority, nor private individuals, who wish to see their business interests furthered, are prepared to acknowledge that the social right to communicate may be exercised by organizations such as cooperatives, trade unions, churches, social movements or human rights, environmentalist, women's, indigenous or ethnic minority groups. So we find governments and private firms coming to agreements, which are then transformed into broadcasting laws, that actually exclude civil society by declaring illegal media that spring up spontaneously or otherwise barring the way to any kind of involvement by social movements in mass communication.

Thus the field of communication becomes a closed shop, dominated by the political authorities or the power of money. The private media, always quick to defend the free flow of information and communication, are the first to oppose the legalization of media emerging from social and popular organizations, which not only compete for the audience, but question the social and economic policies which the media corporations uphold. Nor are authoritarian governments which are committed to following structural adjustment policies imposed by international financial institutions prepared to pay the political cost of allowing popular opposition media to question their actions.

The right to communicate is a fundamental right because it opens the way to the exercise of other human rights. Beyond the right to inform and be informed, it includes the community's right to break the silence imposed upon it, to form opinions and bring political pressure to bear. Full exercise of this right is an essential tool for the empowerment of peoples, since it challenges the efforts of the power elites to manipulate opinion and monopolize the analysis of facts and reality.

Drawing on her own experience in the struggle for the democratization of politics and society in Burma, the 1991

Nobel Peace Prize-winner Aung San Suu Kyí suggests that "the true development of human beings involves much more than mere economic growth. At its heart must be a sense of empowerment and inner fulfilment. This alone will ensure that human and cultural values remain paramount in a world where political leadership is often synonymous with tyranny and the rule of a narrow elite. People's participation in social and political transformation is the central issue of our time."[3]

Such participation includes the right to communicate, but people also require this right simply in order to express their dignity. If a people is to have a sense of its worth and feel respected, it must be able to make its ideas and actions known publicly via channels ranging from group media and theatre to audiovisual media and the information superhighway. To command a public hearing is undoubtedly the aim of every individual and group wishing to put across its message effectively and with dignity.

If something practical is to be done, access to the public sphere must be part of political aims pursued by democratic forces in society. A member of the National Forum for the Democratization of Communication in Brazil, Fernando Sa, suggests that democratic sectors must adopt "an aggressive attitude in order to make up the ground they have lost, whether by... engaging in a relentless struggle at the institutional level to have the prevailing model restructured or, in bold support of civil society initiatives, by disputing the control of communication today."[4]

Cees Hamelink points out that the prevailing communication system is not neutral but that corporations are taking over a public space and turning it into a private one. The "electronic superhighway", he warns, "is too important to be left to the laws of the market or in state hands. We have to create an electronic future in which everyone counts. We can't say No to the superhighway, because it is going to happen in any case, but we have to fight for it to be controlled by civil society. The churches must also be present in the current negotiations on telecommunications."[5]

Communication and human rights

As we saw earlier, Rwanda is a case in point of an authoritarian state using rigid control of the means of communication to violate human rights systematically. The situation in Argentina during the military dictatorship of the 1970s, which was responsible for thousands of murders and 30,000 "disappeared", also illustrates how local elites use privatized media to back the lies propagated by the authorities and imposed by repression. During the 1978 World Cup in Argentina a private radio launched a campaign whose slogan was "*Los Argentinos somos Derechos y Humanos*" ("We Argentinians are straight and humane") to counteract what the military called the "anti-Argentinian campaign abroad". It claimed charges of human rights violations made by sources as diverse as the Carter administration in the USA, the countries of what is now the European Union, Amnesty International, Americas Watch and the WCC were gross "fabrications" designed to ruin the country's "prestige". One women's magazine usually devoted to recipes and fashion (and now owned by one of Argentina's biggest multimedia concerns) printed the slogan on postcards, which its readers were encouraged to send to international forums and human rights organizations to show that all was well in Argentina, and that tortures, deaths and disappearances were only a fiction put out by foreigners.

This is behind Hamelink's warning that campaigns against censorship should not attack only governments, because private firms constitute an even bigger threat. "Private operators," he says, "always talk about free flow, but when someone like Rupert Murdoch wants to transmit via satellite to China, and the Chinese are worried about the BBC because 'it may give our people the wrong ideas', Murdoch replies that 'China's a big market, and it won't go to the BBC.' Market logic takes precedence over freedom of expression and the free flow of information and communication."[6]

Combined action by government and media owners is presently thwarting people's right to communicate in El Salvador. After the end of a ten-year civil war that caused something like 100,000 deaths, a group of rural communities decided to set up their own media to bear witness to their situation and work for peace and democratic change. The medium they opted for was local radio, and they refused to allow their own political leaders to influence editorial policies. They did not want to serve as a mouthpiece for others, but to reflect their own pluralism.

"We wanted to establish independent media that were impartial, objective and true. Our commitment is to the people, to enable them to become the active promoters of their human dignity," says Lorenzo de Jesús Mungia of the Board of Community Radios of El Salvador.[7] "We broadcast the voices of those who have been silenced, and we work to make our radios platforms for rural planning and organization. Our chief aim is to serve the people, not to make use of them." Local communities in El Salvador know little about human rights, which the military dictatorship wrested from them. The radios highlight this theme since, even with the peace agreements, the government, large landowners and industrialists do not respect the people's right to exercise their citizenship in freedom.

The community radios decided to unmask the lies propagated by the official line. "We knew they were going to harass us and try to close us down in any case, so we decided to tell the truth about the violations and seek support," continues Mungia. "Unfortunately the peace agreements have not changed the poverty, insecurity and neglect. Repression continues. To condemn it we are using the voice of the people rather than professionals."

For these radios, building democracy in El Salvador means making sure that people know about and understand the peace agreements. "The radios are trying to work together so that we can close this dark chapter of our history and turn a new page," says Mungia. The task is therefore to monitor compliance with the agreements on a day-to-day basis, and campaign for them to be made law. Keeping track of the process is one way the rural communities can contribute to strengthening democracy.

But this kind of conscientization is not to the taste of those in power. Five closure orders plus heavy fines are hanging over the community radios. "Our government is punishing us for arousing people's interest and increasing the level of participation. The closure orders are an attack on the dignity of our people."

Clearly, for governments and elites used to controlling the lives and minds of their people, any communication that creates awareness is dangerous. They prefer a "communication of forgetfulness" like that described by Guatemalan communicator Carlos Aldana.[8] Aldana believes that "in a country like ours the historical memory needs to be strengthened…" This does not mean clinging to a "vengeful memory", but it is wrong to talk of "reconciliation without memory". In all Latin American countries which suffered under repressive military dictatorships, governments elected by the people and the media are now calling for reconciliation. Little is said of the need for justice. "As Christian communicators we must keep both themes going," says Aldana. "We prefer to talk of reconciliation rather than justice because the message is easier, and… it seems more Christian…"

But people are sometimes ready to defend the media that represent them. According to Sung-ho Cho of the Christian Broadcasting Service (CBS) in South Korea, his network has been persecuted by government for telling the truth. Despite threats and repression, the radio has managed to make a name for itself with listeners. "Almost all the media in my country curry favours with those in power," says Cho, "but our station takes a different stand. The public recognizes that we broadcast the truth about what is going on. CBS is recognized as a credible medium not only in church, but also in secular circles. It has an impact in Korean society. People wait to hear our news because they know they will be properly informed."[9]

CBS has 80 reporters in the field and 50 radio producers. "People who work for CBS are committed to the truth," affirms Sung-ho Cho. "As Christian communicators, we understand that this is an ethical commitment. If we fulfil it we can endure the problems. And our audience protects us. If the government tried anything against us now it would have to face public opinion; people would protest."

In many countries democracy exists only in a formal sense. Some Latin American thinkers call these "low-intensity democracies" — or worse, national security democracies". [10] These governments claim to be democratizing, but continue to endorse repression appropriate to the doctrine of national security. Human rights are still violated, and the power of a minority is imposed on the majority of the population. "Democracy" is divorced from human rights, and the mass media play an important part in psychological warfare whose "primary purpose is to spread despair". The impunity for the crimes of the military and other agencies of repression, says Hinkelhammert, "creates a feeling of not having guaranteed rights, of not being recognized as a person by the state which, though democratically elected, continues to be terrorist." [11]

It is not easy to rebuild a sense of community when people have lived for decades under dictatorial and repressive regimes. If human rights are to be fully enforced, people need to learn about these rights, understand how to defend them and be ready to put them into practice in their own everyday relations.

A training centre in Soweto, South Africa, working on communication for human dignity, asked young people to describe the human rights situation in their own community in photo and video material. According to Keromamang Mapheto of the South African Communication and Development Institute, which coordinated the project, "the youth took pictures of the kind of housing most people live in, which deprives them of human dignity. They highlighted other aspects of their life: despair caused by unemployment, the degradation of families who do not have enough to eat, the street children..." [12] Keromamang observes that before South Africa's transition to a non-racial democracy, "the laws would not allow us to be in groups greater than five people, and we were not given the chance to use communication... There is a lot to do now so that people can build up effective communication, which can nourish their life."

The Soweto group found they could express their view of what was happening in their community through photography. In a country where the right of assembly has long been denied, it was vital to begin with group media in order to create community. "The Council of Churches has encouraged people to work together. This has to do with transmitting information, but also with work for unity. People have to learn who they are, gain self-respect, and recover their own dignity. All these things were stolen from them during the years of apartheid," says Keromamang.

This task should not be underestimated. "Empowering people at the grassroots level is a formidable task. Organizations and individuals are called to put all their creative and technical skills at the service of the disenfranchised, the disempowered, the dehumanized and outcast."[13]

The limits of poverty

In countries where most of the population lives below the poverty line and even basic needs are not met, the free flow of information is impossible. This is not only because the basic communication structures do not exist, but also because poverty is generally accompanied by mass illiteracy.

Today almost a 1000 million people around the world are illiterate, and of those, 70 percent are women. Around 150 million children have no chance of going to school. The chief difficulty for many illiterate people is access to the information they need to solve their most important problems and meet their basic needs. "Wherever we are in the world, regardless of our cultural context, we require the information and the intellectual environment conducive to thinking and decision-making... We need the literacy skills to enable us to create and to understand the appropriate symbols for documentation and dissemination of our ideas... In a world of rapid technological transformation in the means of communication, dispossessed people have in common an urgent need to be heard and supported in their efforts to recover even fragments of their shattered human dignity."[14]

Drawing on a study of the links between war and poverty, Frances D'Souza notes that in 1993, 52 wars were going on around the world in 42 countries; in 37 other countries the level of political violence was enough to create an atmosphere of endemic social conflict. Of these 89 countries gripped by war and confrontation, 65 were in the Third World, 55 of them on the lowest step of the global human development index.[15]

Poverty and illiteracy go hand in hand. Dealing with a population whose dignity and rights have been violated, those in power may take decisions that lead to further subjection, new wars and still greater suffering. In Rwanda the chief victims of media manipulation were poor and illiterate. It is easier to abuse the human rights of such people, including their right to communication and information. Can we conclude that it suits some power elites to keep the people in a state of poverty, thus ensuring that their own power will not be challenged?

Structural adjustment programmes imposed by the International Monetary Fund have produced increased poverty and widened the gap between rich and poor, between the information-rich and the information-poor. Those with the know-how and technologies at their disposal keep these to themselves. "Apartheid in technology and in knowledge is just as perverse as social apartheid," says the Jesuit priest Xavier Gorostiaga.[16] The concentration of knowledge is a new factor in the global struggle for power, further eroding the right of poor peoples to dignity. Analyzing the policies of exclusion caused by the globalization of world markets, Gorostiaga points out that whole populations are treated as if they were "superflous" and left without any hope of development. The doctrine of globalization encourages the development of a "cognitive elite" whose intellectual achievements justify their aspirations to power in the new technological society. On this view, it makes no sense for the state to invest in training the poorly qualified. Scholarships should go to the highly gifted who are more likely to produce dividends in the form of technological progress. In this scenario, knowledge and information will become even more unattainable for most of the world's people, and power will be even more highly concentrated than at present.

At this point the need to democratize communication is clearly a matter of justice. Equal opportunities of access to education, information and knowledge are fundamental to building human dignity. Working for democracy is more than having free access to giving and receiving information; it also involves the opportunity to use that information to challenge and limit the excesses of the powerful and to fight for the rights and the quality of life of those whom the present system persists in excluding.

Participation in democracy

No one expects the mass media to invite participation by the different sectors of society, nor to become the entirely disinterested voice of minorities. But the media *can* fulfil a representative role in response to their audience's needs. Latin American researcher Jesús Martin Barbero comments that people use the media to air their grievances and express social protest in direct, practical ways. [17] They know that when these are broadcast to the whole country and even abroad, authorities will have to listen and, very probably, a solution will be found more quickly than by any other means.

Research on Italian radio and television found that certain media personalities had acquired a representative capacity unequalled by any politician. People turned to the former when they wanted to bring a problem to the government's attention, certain that they would get a more rapid response than if they entrusted their concern to the political bureaucracy.

In formal "democracies" like Argentina the media are often used for their representative capacity. Whenever there is a need to put traffic lights at a dangerous intersection, or to improve public safety, or to preserve a park or public square that commercial interests are trying to privatize, the neighbourhood will stage a protest, blocking streets, carrying placards, with plenty of loud music. The aim is to capture the interest of radio microphones and television cameras. Spokespersons will explain the situation, demand the attention of local government representatives, berate officials. Citizens know this is the surest way to make themselves heard, and that the authorities will have to find a solution to the problem if they are not to be exposed again for their negligence.

For their part, the media can be sure that their news will be followed by the whole local community, and many others who identify with it. The success of the protest will encourage others like it, and the mobile transmitters will be warmly welcomed at each local demonstration. The citizens allow their social protest to be turned into a show in order to achieve their aims; this in turn reinforces the influence of the media.

The public may also turn against the media when it thinks the truth has been distorted and concealed. At the beginning of the uprising in the Mexican state of Chiapas in January 1995, the Mexican media presented a view that was contradicted by the European media also covering events in Chiapas. When Mexican public opinion became aware that it was being misinformed, its vote of no-confidence in the biggest national multimedia was reflected in a significant drop in audience figures. Manipulation was impossible because people demanded to know the truth. A huge popular demonstration of support for the indigenous movement filled Mexico City's Zocalo Square under the watching eyes of the world's media, and undoubtedly saved the Zapatista Army of National Liberation (EZLN) from military action.

By using the Internet to issue its communiqués and call for international solidarity and support, the EZLN brought the indigenous movement into the modern world. [18] While many individuals, movements and organizations have already taken advantage of this high-tech facility to work for peace, justice, human rights, environmental concerns and democracy, this was the first time a people's army was able to publicize its thinking by way of tools that were once the preserve of the military, governments, corporations and banks. Interactive communication through the electronic media ensured transparency (the EZLN's detailed proposals were sent by electronic mail to the world's press) and helped to speed up the peace talks.

Dialogue is possible between indigenous cultures and the electronic media, if communication respects peoples' right to self-determination.

Earlier we mentioned the important role of community radios. Latin America and the Spanish-speaking Caribbean have a long history in this field. With 90 broadcaster members throughout the region, the Latin American Association for Radio Education (ALER) has been working for 25 years to strengthen the links between radios and popular organizations in order to reach the widest possible range of sectors of society. ALER's work was born out of a school radio experiment sponsored by the Roman Catholic Church. Substantial airtime was given to popular education and communication, and "our work was linked with popular organizations from the start", says Eloy Arribas of ALER. "We contacted miners, small farmers, young people, women, so that movements demanding basic economic and civil rights would get a hearing." [19]

ALER establishes an egalitarian relationship with the communities it serves. "People are part of the process of communication," affirms Arribas. "We should be ready to provide training and continuous advice." Rather than preaching to the converted, the idea is to attract the biggest possible audience. Training is backed by audience surveys to test the impact of the broadcasts. These stations are focussing mainly on democracy and citizens' rights. They try to facilitate encounter between different sectors of society, and between people's groups and the authorities. The purpose of communication is fulfilled as the community begins to make its views count when decisions affecting their well-being are being taken.

But the possibility of greater involvement in the media is not always put to good use. There has recently been an opening in this direction in Ghana, and churches have applied to obtain licences to operate their own media, particularly radio stations. Emmanuel Bortey from a local Christian publishing company says that "unfortunately, in my country there is no real conscious effort to appreciate the role of the media and to learn to be critical". Tabloids of all kinds are currently proliferating, and "sometimes people are at a loss to interpret or understand the information they are getting, because they have been used to taking everything that is printed as the truth". In the new press situation, the churches "should make some attempt to make use of the media wisely, for socialization, for evangelization, for creating awareness, for reaching the remoter areas of the country. Churches need to use the media for sustainable development," Bortey says. [20]

According to the seventh MacBride Round Table (Tunisia, March 1995), democratization of the media in Africa depends on the existence of a "viable civil society organized in citizens' groups, social movements, human rights and women's organizations... Democracy declines and may disintegrate when its processes are usurped by politicians and their parties." New openings to the media offer interesting opportunities for churches and Christian groups to contribute to the establishment of full democracy. Will Africa's churches and Christian communicators take advantage of them?

The key role played by Christians in the democratizing process in South Africa is well known. Keromamang Mapheta recalls that "we did not see what we could do as part of government. We had to start educating ourselves first... It was amazing the way people started to be educated in democracy. We still have many questions coming up, but young people especially now have open eyes and are critical of the things they come across. I believe that after five years of democratic experience we will know exactly what we need."

Democratizing the media will require substantial change in another area, as was underlined by 450 women communicators from 80 countries who met in Bangkok in 1994 for a world congress on "Women Empowering Communication". They questioned the attempts of commercial mass media to turn individuals into consumers not only of goods but also of patriarchal ideas and ideologies, and called for "gender sensitivity in the communication field".

Complaints about the media's devaluation of women's roles and use of women's images for commercial purposes, or about the small number of women on media decision-making bodies, need to be backed up by steady work for a new gender-sensitive approach, the congress said. The declaration from the Bangkok congress suggested that women and men can work together to incorporate "humane values such as harmony with nature, cooperation, nurturing, caring, love and compassion, into our media creations and our struggles for freedom, to ensure that our alternatives do not become hierarchical, undemocratic and elitist".

As Noeleen Heyzer has pointed out, "making a pro-gramme from a 'woman's point of view' means something more than simply being sympathetic to women. Basically, it could affect either the choice of subject-matter, or the way the subject-matter is handled, or both. On some occasions it might mean that the camera is placed behind the woman so that the audience literally sees events from her position. On other occasions a woman might be the protagonist of the story: she initiates the action, asks the questions and provides the answers... It might mean that the viewer is clearly addressed as a woman and not simply as part of a family."[21]

A Jamaican group called "Women's Media Watch" has been working with readers, viewers and listeners to "decode" sexist messages in the media, and with professionals to look at how they report the news. Michelle Golding leads work-shops in which professionals — both men and women — from alternative and mainstream media discuss gender issues. According to Golding, "we find that men are con-cerned about sexism and are willing to listen even if they do not agree with all our perspectives. We want people to analyze what is going on in the media... and to propose policy changes on content."[22]

If half the world's population is kept in a position of subjection, silence and invisibility, there is little hope of constructing a democracy in which the dignity of all men and women is respected. It is essential to recover those values that patriarchalism dismisses as "women's business", and recognize their importance. Kamla Bhasin enumerates these values: "nurturing, caring, selflessness, being emotional, being like nature, creative, non-violent, non-linear, non-specialized, circular". These values "have been labelled feminine and therefore looked down upon, marginalized or crushed... The killing of the feminine is what has made our world today so inhuman. We need to affirm these feminine values."[23]

But feminine values are not restricted to women. They have simply have been labelled as such by patriarchal power when, in reality, they belong to the whole of humanity, women and men alike. Putting them into practice will be essential for building a democracy in which equality of opportunities and justice are a reality.

NOTES

[1] Mario Vargas Llosa, "La Voz de Dios", *La Nación* (daily newspaper), Buenos Aires, 8 Jan. 1996.
[2] "Conclusions and recommendations, IV: Democratization of Communication," in *Many Voices, One World*.
[3] Aung San Suu Kyí, "Democracy — The Common Heritage of Humanity", *Media and Development*, Vol. 42, no. 3, 1995, p.3.
[4] Fernando Sa, "Comunicación y Democracia", in L. Mendes, ed., *Comunicación, Cultura y Cambio Social en el Marco del Mercosur*, Sao Paulo, WACC-Latin America, 1994, p.107.
[5] Cees Hamelink, presentation in Metepec.
[6] *Ibid.*
[7] Lorenzo de Jesús Mungia, presentation in the panel "Latin America: from reflection to action" in Metepec, and in an interview for this book.

8 Carlos Aldana, "Comunicación para la Dignidad Humana", keynote address to the WACC-Central America congress, Guatemala City, July 1995.

9 Sung-ho Cho, interview for this book at Metepec.

10 Franz J. Hinkelammert, *Cultura de la esperanza y sociedad sin exclusión*, San José, DEI, 1995, p.122.

11 *Ibid.*, p.129.

12 Keromamang Mapheto, interview for this book at Metepec.

13 From the report of the issue group on human rights at Metepec.

14 From Hopeton Dunn's keynote address in Metepec.

15 Frances D'Souza, lecture on "Communication and Peace" in Metepec.

16 Xavier Gorostiaga, S.J., "Citizens of the Planet and of the 21st Century", lecture at the UN Social Summit, Copenhagen, March 1995; published in *CRIE Bulletin*, no. 124, June 1995.

17 Jesús Martin Barbero, "Culturas Populares e Identidades Políticas", in *Entre públicos y ciudadanos*, Lima, Asociación de Comunicadores Sociales Calandria, 1994, p.30.

18 Samuel Ruiz, lecture at Metepec (on tape).

19 Eloy Arribas, interview for this book at Metepec.

20 Emmanuel Bortey, interview.

21 Noeleen Heyzer, "Women, Communication and Development: Changing Dominant Structures", *Media and Development*, Vol. 41, no. 2, 1994.

22 Michelle Golding, interview for this book at Metepec.

23 Kamla Bahsin, keynote speech, "Women Empowering Communication — From Bangkok to Beijing" at Metepec.

3. Culture, Identity and People's Struggles

"Culture" is a multidimensional concept that encompasses a people's values, attitudes, rules of society, traditions, relationships and behaviours, as well as their language and creative expressions. Culture is part of the communication process, of its methods and structure, just as communication, whether interpersonal or group, modern or traditional, verbal or non-verbal, is the principal vehicle for transmitting cultural values and traditions. Scholars of cultural phenomena have maintained that communication is at the heart of a nation's cultural identity, since it is cultural values that provide the symbolic links that create and preserve social cohesion. [1] The individual and collective identity of persons and peoples are forged in the medium of culture.

But culture is not a static medium that produces a "frozen" identity. Identity is shaped in a dynamic process involving day-to-day changes. It can never exist only in terms of tradition, for it is also bound up with a people's present and future.

What is the relationship between the mass communication media, culture and people's identities? Is it a destructive or an enriching one? Some wish to preserve static identities from contact with the outside world, or from change of any kind now or in the future. Nevertheless, "by communicating with others, we communicate with ourselves — provided, of course, that it is a genuine interchange, a real two-way dialogue, an encounter between cultures, not a case of the absorption of some by others... If all identities draw on symbols and myths rooted in the social imagination, then the mass media, in the interests of greater social cohesion, could and should be part of any identity-building process." [2]

One positive aspect of our world is its cultural diversity. For one thing most people seem to agree that this makes an international community a more interesting place than one that is culturally monolithic. At the same time, in looking at identity we should take care not to provoke divisions among the various cultural groups within societies and nations. The mass media should transmit voices and images from other-than-dominant cultures which have something positive to

42

contribute to their respective societies from their particular life-styles, cultural expressions, work, thought and spirituality.

Christian communicators from the Middle East met in 1995 to discuss the possibility of using satellite communications to broadcast the message of the gospel. The debate was intense. Ethnic, cultural and religious balances are delicate in this region. Local Christians feared that this initiative — considered by its Western Christian promoters as "the most strategic opportunity in the history of mission to the Middle East" — might become an obstacle to interfaith dialogue. Jews and Muslims might interpret it as a new invasion by the West, another crusade, this time using new technologies and international mass media instead of military force.

After extensive discussion, the participants concluded that broadcasts of the Christian message in a region where satellite dishes are gaining in popularity every day would be a good thing. But they insisted that viewers who are not Christians should not get the impression of being treated as potential converts. On the contrary, the programming should be highly respectful of the region's other religions. It should bear only indirect witness to faith in Jesus Christ, by reporting on the life of the churches in the region and in the world, and by affirming interfaith dialogue in the region.

"It is natural that within this multi-cultural and multi-religious atmosphere, where religious minorities such as Christians and Jews live in a sea of Muslims who are divided among themselves and do not 'speak with one voice', the simplest difficulty in communication may lead to misunderstandings, be perceived as provocative and lead, in reaction, to a... self-defensive reflex on the part of the other groups," says the headmistress of an Armenian school in Beirut, Manoushag Boyadjian. "A wrong assessment may, and has in the past, led the Muslim majority to equate the indigenous Christians, who have dwelt in these lands since the time of Pentecost, and whom they have known for centuries, with the West, which is perceived as an alien Christian entity, a traditional enemy of Islam, whose aim is to dislodge them from the eastern shores of the Mediterranean."[3]

Fortunately, says Boyadjian, the option of dialogue, aiming at mutual understanding and reciprocal enrichment, does exist. Christian-Muslim discussions centre not only on cooperation in humanitarian services and human rights, but also on equality and freedom, the definition of citizenship, justice and peace in the region. "These discussions are extremely encouraging because both parties want to move from a position of reaction to one of action... They will yield results, provided they aim at breaking barriers," she affirms. "Many Christians and Muslims have become convinced that dialogue is the only alternative to violence, as well as a necessary means to exchange knowledge and information, to rediscover and highlight a common past, common ethical and spiritual values, to promote new standards and criteria for common living, to strengthen the sense of belonging to the same society, the same region, and to cooperate in matters of common destiny."

In Ghana, where Christians make up 60 percent of the population, Muslims 25 percent, and the rest belong to traditional religions, there is also need for dialogue on cultural and religious issues. "Though there are no formal indigenous religious structures in Ghana, there have been strains between traditional culture and the Christian faith," says Christian publisher Emmanuel Bortey. "There are situations in which traditional norms seem in conflict with Christian values. Christians have had difficulty trying to observe some taboos and traditional requirements that are at variance with their Christian convictions. Unfortunately, there has been no real attempt to find a solution, to look for a compromise."[4]

As far as relations between Muslims and Christians in Ghana are concerned, the churches try to promote dialogue, to get Christians to live in harmony with Muslims. "The difficulty is that Muslim fundamentalist groups in Ghana have a tendency to intolerance. Unfortunately, clashes have occurred," Bortey reports. "But at a formal level, the national council of churches, the Catholic bishops' conference and the national council of Muslims maintain lines of communication. They have made common statements on national issues to show cooperation and acceptance of each other. It is good to work together at a formal level, for this helps us to intervene when there are misunderstandings at the grassroots level."

In Africa, large sectors of society still lack access to the mass media. So group and community media are important in education and communication for dialogue and democracy. Regrettably, traditional means of communication are not generally encouraged by the churches. "There has been a reluctance to focus on... meetings, dances, songs, drama, story-telling and other inter-personal means of communication."[5] These will need to be rehabilitated and placed at the service of religiously and culturally plural African societies.

Radio broadcasting contributed to the development of religious pluralism in Italy. The country was plunged into war by a fascist government under which dissent was unthinkable; after the war it remained under the religious sway of the Roman Catholic Church. But in 1944 the allied powers imposed religious pluralism in state radio. Since then, Radiotelevisione Italiana (RAI) has broadcast a weekly Protestant religious programme in which different denominations cooperate, thus demonstrating their ecumenism and bearing common witness in a predominantly Catholic society. The programme has a large audience. According to Protestant radio and television producer Gianna Urizio, this is because "Protestants are reputed to be progressive on controversial issues".[6] Besides Bible stories and study, the programme covers Italy's political, social and economic problems. Issues such as corruption, abortion and religious education are analyzed by experts from Protestant churches. The ability to project a clear religious identity has undoubtedly been one of the programme's successes.

But an even greater role in building political, social and religious pluralism in Italy has been played by community radio stations. At one time there were as many as 7000 independent radio stations in the country, where you could hear the voices of trade union officials, cooperative members, women, gays and people of various political persuasions and cultural expressions.

Protestants offer a wide variety of such radio programmes. Pentecostals tend to use radio for evangelism, while the Methodist, Lutheran and Waldensian churches cover social topics and allow space for groups like Amnesty International and Greenpeace, students, housewives, the elderly and the unemployed. Some 60 Protestant community radio stations have formed an association aiming at legalization of community radio; it also provides training in programme content and the technical aspects of broadcasting.

The Federation of Protestant Churches in Italy also has a fortnightly half-hour slot on public television. Information about the Protestant world, both national and international, is complemented with coverage of social and political issues — such as the use of public funds, ethics in politics and immigration laws. The Federation tries to present a broad vision of the oikoumene — the situation of the churches in South Africa, Mexico, Latin America and Eastern Europe, for instance. "Italy is culturally a very provincial country that is now opening up to the rest of the world... And Protestants, a religious minority, are contributing to this important cultural, social and political development," Urizio says.

Identity is also bound up with self-determination and cultural independence. Commenting on Radio and Television Martí — the religious radio and television broadcasts to Cuba from the US — Noel Fernández, editor of the *Correo Bautista* and director of the committee of differently-abled persons for the Ecumenical Council of Cuba, says that "this way of manipulating communications has a profound impact. The mission of the church is to proclaim the good news by all possible means, but what is coming here is disinformation disguised as the gospel message. This is alienating, and seeks to come between Cuban Christians and their social and civil responsibilities. These messages are irrelevant to the people of a country grappling with backwardness, poverty and hunger... Most churches are opposed to this type of pseudo-Christian message reaching us from abroad. These programmes... are designed principally to subvert the internal order and create chaos in our society... They do not create community, they divide."[7]

The Ecumenical Council of Cuba is trying to ensure that the Christian message heard in Cuba is one that originates within Cuba. Since 1990, after protracted negotiations with the government, Christian churches have been allowed 30 minutes of air-time free of cost on national radio and on radios in several of the 14 provinces, for specific religious occasions such as Christmas and Easter. The Council has a bimonthly programme on a Havana radio station, but due to poor technical quality it has only a small audience, and the Council hopes to negotiate with government for better facilities for its radio ministry.

Apart from the mass media, the Cuban churches have a number of regular publications with a wide circulation among believers, including the *Heraldo Episcopal*, the *Correo Bautista*, the *Evangelista Cubano*, the *Heraldo Cristiano* and the Cuban Presbyterian Young People's review. The Catholic Church, too, has a Sunday paper that is distributed after mass. The Protestant publications strongly reaffirm Cuban cultural identity and, in general, examine the thinking of great national heroes like José Martí from a liberating Christian perspective.

The loss of traditional values is a recurring theme in the Pacific. Eseteri Kamikamika, chairperson of an ecumenical women's group in Fiji, says "there was more communication with our traditional leadership. A chief is a chief only because of the people. They advise him... With new democratic values, new people who are not chiefs are being elected to parliament, and the communities wonder how they work their leadership... We must make good decisions in order to be helpful to the people. But we cannot do this unless we are informed and aware, unless we believe in communication. Many think that silence means consensus. But in the Pacific, people are used to thinking things through together before making a decision. New, young chiefs who are not familiar with the traditions have to be informed."[8]

"We want to be independent," Kamikamika continues, "but we need to train our people for decision-making... Many are Christians, but do not yet relate their faith to values and life-styles. We need to stimulate this, and recover spirituality."

Language, culture, identity

The globalization of markets is standardizing consumption, thus changing the way people dress, eat, entertain and express themselves, levelling out differences. The media foster this process. Yet as we have seen, the relationship between people and the media is dialogical; although the transmitter of the message has more power than the receiver, this power is not absolute. By interacting with their audiences, the media can be very useful in both practical and symbolic ways.[9]

"Rap" music, originating in the marginalized youth culture of large US cities, has reached the whole world thanks to the mass media. It has raised awareness of these young people's experience of drugs, racism and violence. And it has asked questions about a system hitherto presented as a gilded model worthy of imitation. A popular cultural expression has become known and visible to a society whose official political and cultural discourse excludes or simply ignores the lives and feelings of its composers. This has also made an impact on local rock groups in Argentina. One of them, Illya Kuriakin, wrote a Quechua rap about the destruction of the indigenous world and the need to restore the dignity of indigenous culture. The Quechua are the largest ethnic group in Argentina, and represent a significant proportion of the population of Bolivia and Peru as well. Because of the globalization of communication, a rhythm born in the urban areas of the North is expressing the protest of a largely rural indigenous population in the South.

A people's cultural identity is closely tied to its language. Colonized areas have had the language of the colonizers imposed on them by force. A colleague from the Pacific recalls that, in his region, pupils were punished if they did not speak in English at school. In Latin America the colonizers destroyed ancient codices that were the key to understanding indigenous art and culture. Imposition of language went hand in hand with political and economic domination, which continues today: entire populations and ethnic groups are excluded from power if they do not use the language of the rulers.

"All peoples have an identity, and this is supported by their... historical and traditional experiences, as well as their means of resisting attempts to exterminate their identity," says Embert Charles, who directs the Folk Research Centre in St Lucia. "A whole life of resistance... influences your identity!" [10]

Most of the people on this small Caribbean island speak Creole, but it is not recognized by the state. By law only English-speakers can become members of parliament. Even the statutes of the Banana Association, whose members are mainly Creole-speaking farmers, stipulate that its representatives should be able to speak English. The whole society is marginalized by the mass media on account of language. Reporters write about people's issues, but miss out information or perceptions because they do not know Creole. "By marginalizing people for their language, we are really undermining their dignity," Charles argues. "They are ashamed to speak their language. There was a time when anyone who spoke Creole in town was called a hick... So people are forced to speak incorrect English, but if you speak bad English in an English-speaking environment, you do not feel part of it anyway."

St Lucia, like many other countries where indigenous languages have been forbidden or denigrated, and indigenous people dehumanized in the process, should be considered a bilingual country. Bilingual education, with books and teaching materials, is essential. The mass media should be bilingual.

But these goals will not be realized without clear government policies. Certainly the market will not make up for their absence. In Paraguay Coca Cola advertises in Guaraní — an indigenous language more widely spoken than the official Spanish. This is not the result of a sudden cultural awareness on the part of a large transnational corporation. It is simply the way to reach a large consumer market. But leaving the field open to the "invisible hand" of the market results in greater injustice towards and exclusion of indigenous peoples.

Efforts to enable communities to build a better future for themselves should recognize and integrate the most important elements of their cultures and traditions. As a result of domination by the white population of Spanish origin, indigenous people in Central America feel embarrassed about their origins. In El Salvador and Guatemala, community radio stations are providing opportunities for indigenous peoples to express themselves. But they will also have to start trusting the mass media, which *can* serve them in putting across their views and awakening their own awareness.

In the Caribbean, where national territorial limits seem to have vanished with the advance of satellite communication, television has created a visual literacy. "Meaning... does not come out of tradition or formal education anymore, but from television. TV has a significant impact on people's worldview," says Embert Charles. He argues that since foreign audiovisual mass media and their impact cannot be kept out, because of the technology, "we must increase our own capacity to put images on TV. Secondly, we have to develop people's capacity to be critical of their consumption of media products. This has to be done not only with adults, but also in schools. And then, at a political level, we need legislation to deal with these issues properly."

Cultural and linguistic domination and discrimination are not confined to the communications media and the educational or political system. Christine Greenaway, a media consultant for the United Church of Canada, says her church has made great efforts to communicate with and for human dignity with French-speaking members and aboriginal people. [11] But the results have not been altogether satis-factory.

"Our French-speaking members, a small minority, prob-ably consider that they are not part of the whole church, because their language is not sufficiently respected," Green-away says. "At a recent national assembly, for instance, we had simultaneous translation, but it was not done by a professional. Almost all our documentation is produced in English only. The cost of producing it in French is huge in relation to the number of people we would reach. But I do not think we are doing enough to let people communicate with dignity. If you have to stand up at a national forum and speak broken English, you feel silly, inadequate, childish. That does not help you to feel dignified."

Improving relations with its members from the "First Nations" of Canada has been a long process of learning about their symbols and values. During national council meetings, an aboriginal person with a talking stick now sits on the platform to symbolize the presence and spiritual contribution of the indigenous community.

Popular culture, new technologies

Popular culture affirms people's identity, names their values and is a tool for finding, maintaining and reclaiming social meaning. It provides the social context within which people may live with human dignity. Belonging to the people, particularly impoverished and marginalized people, it is a powerful social force; and defending or promoting the freedom to create and distribute popular culture is action on behalf of human dignity. [12]

Popular culture can challenge the socio-political order and resist incorporation into the consumer society. It can use new technology creatively to support mobilization at the community level. Theatre, song and dance, puppets and marionettes, and popular art are traditional forms of popular expression that have enabled peoples to transmit wisdom and values from one generation to the next. Today these expres-sions can use technology to broadcast their messages to wider audiences. With the cost of new technologies falling, a growing number of marginalized groups will have access to video, desk-top publishing and electronic communication networks.

For the 500th anniversary of the European conquest of America, a popular communication group in Colombia published the history of the conquest in the form of a short story series. A team of young artists presented the conquest from the standpoint of the conquered, with sensitivity, style and humour, thus contributing to a new awareness of the meaning of colonization in Latin America. Popular theatre is an important instrument of communication in the Philippines, and women in particular have expressed their concerns through this medium. Filming their plays on video has enabled wider distribution. Video technology also allowed dozens of groups the world over to participate in the "Five-Minute Project", which brought glimpses of women's lives in many cultures to the UN's Fourth World Conference on Women in Beijing.

It is important for the people involved in such ventures really to be part of the cultural expressions they are recording. Unfortunately, the dominant media do not always take popular culture seriously, and when they do it is more often for commercial gain than interest in cultural values. Popular celebrations like carnival have become outright business ventures whose garish excesses bear little resemblance to the people's festivals out of which they have grown. In the zeal to commercialize everything, deeply-rooted cultural expressions like folk dances and songs, traditional costumes and even religious expressions have quite simply become a show, robbed of the meaning and profound popular symbolism they once embodied.

In recent years computer networks have allowed individuals, groups and organizations around the world to discuss important issues with each other. Thousands of interest and solidarity groups sprang up around the world to discuss through cyberspace the topics of recent United Nations conferences on the environment, human rights, social development, population, housing and the status of women. In certain respects, these networks are horizontal, democratic spaces of communication. For example, using electronic networks, Greenpeace collected millions of signatures condemning the 1995-96 resumption of French nuclear testing in the South Pacific.

To question the cultural implications of these new information technologies is not to question technological progress per se. [13] It is rather to point out that the technologies often end up undermining communication for, although they are interactive, the operating rules and to some extent the content are determined unilaterally, and continue to increase the power of those who already have it. So it is important for civil society to strive to apply the principles of a just communication order to these new technologies while they are still in their infancy. [14]

We have already seen that the information superhighway will not embrace the whole world. It originated in North America, Europe and Japan, and there are no plans for a superhighway that starts out from the developing world, nor for entries or exits in the peripheral regions of the planet. A good part of the world's population will have no access to it.

At the same time, attention should focus on the content of the software packages that the new technology uses. What messages are they sending? Are they inclusive or sexist? Are they discriminatory, or do they open the way to dialogue among races and cultures? Do they enable the community to participate, or are they aimed solely at increased consumption? Do they facilitate democratic communication, or do they impose an authoritarian approach? Other questions must address more practical aspects: who sets and collects the "tolls" on the superhighway? who establishes and polices the "traffic code"? will there be "public transportation" offering equal access to all? The promises of a higher volume of communications flow and its efficiency do not necessarily mean greater equity. [15]

Women have already sounded a note of caution concerning the possibility that these new electronic networks could increase gender bias, further undermining their dignity. Sexual violence and pornography are already commonplace on the Internet. Video games, whose chief users are children and youth, also stress sexual violence.

The MacBride Round Table meeting in Tunis in March 1995 warned that gender discrimination may be "built into the very conceptualization of communication technology; the hierarchical structure and the binary logic of informatics is laden with gender-specific values". The Tunis Statement includes a critique of information technology based on a larger epistemological critique of Enlightenment notions of progress and rationality, embodied in science and technology.

Those working in the field of popular culture should examine the content of the information superhighway, in part to demystify it, and in part to democratize its power and impact. Civil society should formulate strategies for using the new information technologies to serve the interests of the community and its culture, and to counteract any inherent threats to human dignity. Globalizing popular cultural expressions is part of a necessary "globalization from below". [16]

Indigenous perspectives

European colonization of America, Africa, Asia and the Pacific went hand in hand with the subjugation of indigenous communities. This entailed muzzling their cultures, destroying their ecosystems, displacing populations to inhospitable areas, denying their language and their spirituality. In America some of these communities have been living in marginalization and discrimination for over 500 years now. In some cases they were legally segregated and obliged to live outside white society; in others they were assimilated and their identity denied; and in certain extreme cases (like that prevailing under the military dictatorship of General Pinochet in Chile), the law ceased to acknowledge their very existence, with the intention of absorbing them into the "national" identity and dividing up their lands. [17]

In many countries with indigenous ethnic groups, the majority of the population has no awareness of being a multiethnic society. With a tacit, implicit, often even unconscious racism, these societies simply ignore their diversity. All groups are obliged to model themselves on the same cultural patterns and "integrate themselves" into processes with which they do not identify. The few territories remaining in the hands of the indigenous people are disputed between corporations and governments whose aim is to occupy and exploit them as they wish in the name of progress or economic development. Those opposing expropriation are labelled as "ignorant" or "backward".

Meanwhile, the culture industry commercializes whatever is unusual or attractive about indigenous cultures, while ignoring their innate values, such as community life, the quest for balance between human beings and nature, respect for the wisdom of the elders and spirituality.

Yet, as the 20th century draws to a close, there is a sort of breaking-in of indigenous peoples into contemporary history. The commemoration of the 500th anniversary of Europe's conquest of America prompted indigenous communities to organize in order to make their side of the story known, creating a new awareness of historical events. Something similar occurred in Australia on the occasion of the bicentenary of the arrival of the first European immigrants.

"The emergence of the indigenous peoples is happening in a surprising way," comments 1980 Nobel Peace Prizewinner Adolfo Pérez Esquivel. "They were the ones least able to contribute to changing the society. It was said that all they wanted was to preserve their customs and stay exactly as they were. But in assuming the role of agents of their own history, indigenous people have opened the way for other players to take part in the long process of social transformation. They are creating the scope for new factors to come into play: environmental demands, in which issues of survival merge with the demands for justice, the voices of women, who face discrimination under all systems and in all ethnic groups..."[18]

"The indigenous peoples who had no future have progressed from non-communication to communication," says

Bishop Samuel Ruiz. "The Indian's time has now come. History is becoming ours, but the process will not be a quick one."[19] The Zapatista movement in Ruiz' diocese in Chiapas signalled that indigenous people and peasants have lost their fear of repression, and are not inspired by lust for power. They have challenged Mexico's civil society to demonstrate its maturity, and to accept that, beyond the scope of partisan movements, it is important to defend justice, equity and the rights of all peoples.

In Chiapas indigenous people became players in society, able to insist that an authoritarian government put aside repression and come to the negotiating table. As mentioned earlier, they used sophisticated technology to make their claims known and to mobilize the civil society. From group and community communication, which doubtless first served to galvanize their movement, they moved on to computer networks, managing the technological leap forward without reneging on their principles.

The Zapatistas opened the eyes of indigenous groups in other parts of the continent and the world, and efforts are going forward to set up an international indigenous press association to help indigenous peoples to offer their own interpretation of history. The task is all the more urgent because indigenous communities are often fragmented and cut off from each other in urban and rural areas, even within the same countries.

Communication and Christian perspectives

The post-literate and symbolic culture of electronic media challenges a Christianity historically rooted in print media, and confronts it with questions: What can media be expected to do or not do in conveying religious faith? What are the implications of the word becoming an image? What space is there for religion-rooted values in an age of consumerism and secularism? How can religious identity be safeguarded in the face of intolerance in the global communications order?[20]

Christians also need to consider the church's own use of media, the impact of media on the church and on religion, and the church's advocacy of reform of media systems. The visual and electronic age presents Christian communicators with entirely different conditions. Technology, religious pluralism and secularism have put the church in many societies in an unfamiliar minority situation, competing with others for space in public discourse.

Church people sometimes lament the passing of traditional, face-to-face communication patterns. These are important alternatives, but the church needs to come to grips with the electronic media age, not only in its communication strategy and cognitive style but, more significantly, in the content of its message. It needs to reformulate the Christian message in a way that is relevant to the social and cultural environment and can compete in the information marketplace.

The mistake of many churches and Christian groups has been to try to make radio and television into an extension of the pulpit. Instead of trying to strike up a dialogue with the audience, they deliver a sermon. Instead of presenting the gospel simply and directly, they resort to a jargon familiar to members but not to people outside the church. They also tend to perceive the audience as sinners, who must change their lives to accede to the good, as if nothing good can come out of society.

The North American televangelists who were so successful at home and abroad during the 1980s used all the resources of television — lighting effects, sound, camera movement, characterization of the preacher, his wife and family — to provide a spectacular backdrop for worship, while the pastor executed both prayer and sermon to perfection. But at times the show obscured the message of the gospel, or even worse, became the sole message.

A group of members from a Methodist congregation in Buenos Aires went to hear US televangelist Jimmy Swaggart during one of his visits to Argentina several years ago. The next Sunday after church they described the elaborate stage sets, the impeccable lighting, the 800-voice choir, the brass band, Swaggart's charisma and the throngs in attendance. When the pastor asked what Swaggart had preached about, they looked at one another. They could not remember.

The electronic church model is spreading quickly in Latin America. The media represent a point of entry especially for evangelical Christianity. Paradoxically, the preacher's relationship with his audience can be quite personal; he might field telephone questions live on the air, for instance. Or in Peru an interdenominational radio has managed to create a nation-wide ecumenical prayer chain. People meet once a week to pray together around a radio.

Peruvian social researcher Rolando Pérez Vela describes another recent trend in Latin America — the use of modern media technologies *inside* the church. In many places, he says, "people no longer carry a hymn book because the church is equipped with an overhead projector, so they can read the words of the hymns, and with electric guitars, an electric organ, percussion, microphones and speakers. These create a festive, participatory atmosphere. People feel recognized, accompanied as they enter the modern age. They hear the same songs and style of preaching as they hear on the radio. People are used to the electronic media, and feel comforted when they hear the message of the gospel through them." [21]

Christian communication is taking on its own characteristics in each region. A common goal is to enable people to feel part of a community and to respond to the challenges of the contemporary world. Whether through mass, group or community media, churches can create communication networks to pool efforts in defence of human dignity. In the Pacific, for example, the stress has been on the need to strengthen people's capacity to challenge the dominant development model and to question potentially oppressive technologies. "Our young people know they can get media education, challenge the present models and create alternatives. There is a potential for Christians to have a say," affirms Dick Avi from the Pacific Association of WACC. [22]

This was underscored in the active role played by the churches in the campaign against French nuclear testing in the region. The Evangelical Church of French Polynesia organized weekly protest marches and prayer meetings during the 1995-96 tests. "Our struggle is the people's struggle," says Thierry Tapu. "Many people who are not practising Christians were waiting to see the churches' position, for they believe that the churches can champion their cause in favour of respect for life and the environment in this part of the world."[23]

Group and community communication, marches and demonstrations promoting Christian values in defence of life and dignity are important vehicles for proclaiming the gospel and denouncing injustice. Some situations require that churches and Christians work to foster interpersonal relations to overcome discrimination. Very early in the AIDS epidemic, for example, church groups and the ecumenical movement started working to counteract prejudice against people with HIV/AIDS, stressing a spirituality capable of love and compassion in the most difficult circumstances. Christian communication through group, community or the mass media can influence attitudes and build awareness of the need to avoid the exclusion from family or society of persons living with AIDS.

Adan Medrano works with an independent association of Catholic laypersons in the US state of Texas who produced a series of short videos on the challenge of AIDS for Christians which won a prize as the best US Christian programme in 1995. The series documents services that emerged within the US Catholic community over the past decade, and tries to show the spirituality behind such service.

"The topic is a complex one, given its sexual aspects and the political, racist and class factors that surround it," says Medrano. "The fact that the major high-risk group in my country comprises Afro-American and Hispanic women is symptomatic of the problem. This group has least access to information on AIDS prevention, and is most powerless to influence their partner, even as faithful wives. This disease brings out the way in which we behave as community, and this is very difficult to accept."[24]

The video series was filmed in New York, Los Angeles, Houston, a small town and an indigenous reserve in North Dakota. People involved in AIDS prevention and getting families to accept persons living with AIDS were interviewed. "We capture the change that took place after these people got involved," Medrano explains. "They no longer passed judgment, their prejudices diminished and they were ready to devote themselves as brothers and sisters to preserving the dignity of those suffering. We did not use speeches, statistics or experts' opinions. Instead, we let the camera discover the symbolic and revealing aspects. We had no narrator, but let the narrative take shape through the people we interviewed. We were able to show the fight against prejudice and for life in a different dimension."

The task of Christian communication is to reveal the truth in a coherent and understandable manner in its social, personal and spiritual dimensions. Much contemporary communication disinforms, disorients and provokes conflict. There are times when we may feel that all communication spaces have been contaminated, and that there is no scope left for fostering justice, love, and solidarity. Yet Christian communication can serve to restore people's individual and collective dignity, create awareness and open the way for dialogue.

NOTES

[1] S. T. Kwame Baofo, ed., *Communication and Culture: African Perspectives*, Nairobi, WACC-Africa, 1989, p.vi.
[2] Mario Kaplún, "Integración, Comunicación y Culturas en el Marco del Mercosur", in *Comunicación, Cultura y Cambio Social en el Marco del Mercosur*, p.58.
[3] Manoushag Boyadjian, "An Overview of the Situation in the Middle East" at Metepec.
[4] Emmanuel Bortley, interview.

[5] Penina M. Mlama, "Culture, Women and the Media", in *Communication and Culture: African Perspectives*.

[6] Gianna Urizio, interview for this book at Metepec.

[7] Noel Fernández, interview for this book at Metepec.

[8] Eseteri Kamikamika, interview for this book at Metepec.

[9] Rosa María Alfaro, "From Popular Cultures to Political Transformations", *loc. cit.*

[10] Embert Charles, interview for this book at Metepec.

[11] Christine Greenaway, interview for this book at Metepec.

[12] From the report of the issue group on popular culture and communication at Metepec.

[13] *Ibid.*

[14] Ubonrat Siriyuvasak, paper presented at the issue group on communication and new technologies in Metepec.

[15] Honolulu Statement, MacBride Round Table, 1994.

[16] From the issue group on popular culture in Metepec.

[17] Lidia Baltra, paper presented at the issue group on indigenous perspectives in Metepec.

[18] Adolfo Pérez Esquivel, "Diálogo entre los pueblos Latinoamericanos: rescatando nuestra identidad de patria grande", *CRIE*, no. 336, Dec. 1995.

[19] Samuel Ruiz, interview at Metepec.

[20] Issue group on communication and religion in Metepec.

[21] Rolando Pérez Vela, interview for this book at Metepec.

[22] Dick Avi, interview for this book at Metepec.

[23] Thierry Tapu, interview for this book at Metepec.

[24] Adan Medrano, interview for this book at Metepec.

4. Is There a Place for Human Dignity?

As the globalization of markets moves relentlessly ahead, the globalization of communication is enabling the market to export its models of consumption by seducing those at the receiving end into adopting the rules of its game. How many will be left outside is not an issue. The goal is to increase individualism and social fragmentation so that persons come to perceive themselves only as consumers. Individuals, groups and peoples are important according to the level of their involvement in the market. Governments are weak compared to powerful transnational corporations, and the state is losing its identity. Human dignity seems to have been forgotten. The only thing that counts is purchasing power.

If there are alternatives to this, they will not spring out of nowhere. They have to be built, and they will not be built by the powers-that-be but from below, by men and women together seeking answers to the many problems afflicting today's world.

The possibility of a worldwide "globalization from below" is beginning to emerge among ordinary people — the poor, indigenous and marginalized peoples — a movement that can challenge power and say No to exclusion and enslavement. Today we are witnessing the slow but steady growth of a global civil society, prepared to act in solidarity to prevent power from remaining in the hands of a few commercial interests and to work for a new order in which the voices of all the world's inhabitants, linked together internationally in just and equitable economic, political and social relationships, will be heard.

When unscrupulous entrepreneurs secretly imported undocumented workers from Brazil to Argentina to work in slave-like conditions to build prestigious municipal projects, the Argentine construction workers' union joined its counterpart in Brazil to demand compliance with Argentina's labour laws. The media supported the union's campaign, and televised the sub-human living conditions to which these workers were being subjected, for wages 50 percent lower than those of their Argentinian counterparts.

When a ship with radioactive material on board attempted to sail from Europe to Japan, thousands of dock workers in Europe, Africa and North America refused to service it, and were supported by public opinion and governments in a collective refusal to be exposed to nuclear risk. The same resistance was evident in the world campaign against nuclear tests in the South Pacific. The marches and prayers of the Pacific peoples were echoed by marches and prayers across the world, and even by government statements. The strength of feeling around the world caused the French government to be discredited, and persuaded it to end the tests earlier than planned.

When the women's movement began organizing for the UN World Conference on Population and Development in Cairo in 1994, they used all sorts of communication networks, from group to electronic media, to ensure that their defence of women's rights to reproductive health would not be stifled or side-tracked by debate on the abortion issue. This strategy was successful, thanks to the creation of thousands of alternative channels of communication in which public policies could be debated worldwide, free of prejudice and discrimination.

When Bishop Desmond Tutu and the South African churches were fighting against apartheid, they were supported across the world by boycotts, demonstrations and prayer chains. Bishop Samuel Ruiz has now experienced something similar in his campaign for the peace and dignity of the Maya people in Chiapas, a campaign strengthened by the support and prayers of hundreds of thousands of people throughout the world in a communication network inspired by God's Spirit.

These civil communication networks take advantage of technological progress, and strengthen movements for peace, human rights and the environment, which thus become international. Formerly scattered groups now communicate with one another and are building up power from the grassroots.

One of the aims of the organizations forming the Mac-Bride Round Table is to set up alternative structures of communication and public control of the mass media, through mechanisms linked with civil society independently of the state. Global civil society needs to push for the right to "receive and impart information" — referred to in Article 19 of the Universal Declaration of Human Rights — to be replaced by the broader concept of the "right to communication", which implies free democratic interaction in the communications field. "The most diverse sectors of the people must have access to the global communication channels... Active participation in the process of communication lies at the heart of the right to communicate."[1]

This transnational civil communication movement represents an alternative culture, believing that the free market is incapable of responding to people's needs. It promotes worldwide equitable, sustainable and participatory development, in which the priority is quality of life for all. This development model is not based on the accumulation of material goods, indiscriminate consumption and mindless growth (at the cost of plundering natural resources and polluting air and water), but on balance, harmony and just and equitable relationships between peoples.

"The mood at the end of this century encourages us to discard hope as we would a tired horse. But we must not listen to those voices. As soon as we begin communicating with one another, the energy generated by that communication enables us to create a different world, enables us to dare to launch out on the forbidden adventure of freedom. We have been taught a value system according to which we should only do what is profitable. But we do not live to make profits: we live to embrace," says Eduardo Galeano.[2]

To embrace means to be close, to share, to feel in solidarity, to identify with the needs of others. Embracing unites and creates community. It is important to begin to open up new spaces for communication based on solidarity, communication that enables people to embrace.

Radically changing the dominant scientific technological culture, which cannot sustain universal values, human rights and moral standards, means introducing a fundamental change of values. For that to take place, we must move forward from a technocracy that rules over people to a humanization of technology placed at the service of individuals and peoples. We must move on from industrialization that destroys the environment to one that respects harmony and sustainable development, from an immoral to a morally responsible society; from formal democracy to democratic systems in which it is possible for freedom and justice to exist together. [3]

Just as the indigenous movements have succeeded in gaining recognition of their rights to a place at the negotiating table, so also those who desire to see radical changes in how the media are managed must speak out and build alternative models. When the Mexican press was misrepresenting what was happening in Chiapas, Bishop Samuel Ruiz asked journalists at a press conference: "What instructions did your editors give you today? You should stop obeying instructions to misrepresent. As journalists, you should be contributing to peace by reporting the truth." [4]

"Communication is what leads us to Truth and Hope, with all their risks. As Christians, we believe that truth will out. We also believe that change comes from the subjects of change, and not from the subjects of conservation. Change will not come as a gift of the goodwill of the established powers," writes Carlos Aldana of Guatemala. [5] It will come from those whom the system tries to exclude, by way of a "globalization from below" from which the churches and Christian communicators cannot be absent. "And the excluded, with all the power of their fragility, proclaim, 'We are not alone! We have a voice. We are the image of God. We are the majority. We will build hope. We will build our dignity.'" [6]

If human dignity is to be recovered in a world characterized by cold rationalism, immovable laws and statistics that claim to justify the gains of a few at the expense of the many, it will be necessary "to recover the essential elements of human language, which has been, and is still being, savagely torn apart by the culture of specialization and the division of labour."[7] This will mean reviving a *lenguaje sentipensante*, a language of thoughts and feelings. For the community of illiterate fishery workers on the Colombian coast who coined this term in Spanish, this is a language that expresses truth, because it brings mind and heart together again — the world of ideas and the world of feelings.

In the global market system, everything seems cut off from everything else. Reason has been successfully detached from emotion. But we are whole beings who can communicate truthfully only if we can express ourselves in this language of the mind and of the heart. In this language statistics by themselves are irrelevant; what is relevant is the right of women and men to live in dignity.

There *is* a place for human dignity in the system of global communication. But if the voices of all are to be heard, "globalization from below" must be strengthened. It is already coming into being. In it, the Christian message, essentially expressed in the language of the mind and the heart, is evident in actions for life, participation and the dignity of persons and communities.

NOTES

[1] Howard Frederick, "Communication in Contemporary Society", *loc. cit.*
[2] Eduardo Galeano, "Notes on the Media of Incommunication", lecture at Metepec.
[3] Hans Küng, *Global Responsibility: In Search of a New World Ethic*, London, SCM Press, 1991, p.20.
[4] Samuel Ruiz, interview at Metepec.
[5] Carlos Aldana, "Communicación para la dignidad humana", *loc. cit.*
[6] Dennis Smith, "A Latin American Perspective on Human Dignity in Practice", *Media Development*, Vol. 43, no. 1, 1996, p.26.
[7] Eduardo Galeano, *loc. cit.*

Appendix 1

The World Association for Christian Communication (WACC)

The World Association for Christian Communication (WACC) came into being through the merger of three organizations. The World Association for Christian Broadcasting (founded in 1954) united in 1968 with the Coordinating Committee for Christian Broadcasting to form WACC. In 1975 a further merger took place with the Agency for Christian Literature Development. Whereas the World Association for Christian Broadcasting had been concerned with forming policies and encouraging fellowship, the Coordinating Committee for Christian Broadcasting and the Agency for Christian Literature Development had concentrated their efforts on setting up projects and programmes. WACC inherited from those two organizations their concern and responsibility for funding and consultancy as well as their missionary thrust.

With the establishment of WACC, funds from missionary sources were supplemented by contributions from development agencies with the aim of facilitating community and social development projects. Also included — although to a lesser extent — were communication projects of a missionary or evangelistic nature.

WACC is organized in eight regions, which determine the composition of its governing body, the central committee. The central committee focuses on the regions' need for professional guidance and inspiration of members and Christian communicators in general. It also funds communication activities which reflect regional concerns and encourages ecumenical unity among communicators.

WACC's ecumenical nature is evident in its membership and project activities, in its encouragement of grassroots cooperation between Protestant, Orthodox and Roman Catholic communicators, in its challenge to denominational communication activities to seek a broader base and in its search for cooperation among people of different faiths and ideologies.

As a professional organization, WACC serves the ecumenical movement by offering guidance on communication policies, interpreting developments in communications worldwide and discussing their consequences for churches and communities everywhere, especially in the South, and assisting in training Christian communicators and networking.

WACC gives priority to the South, believing that this approach is the most appropriate interpretation of Christ's teaching at this point in history. Six of its eight regions are in the developing world, and funds from missionary and development sources support work in the South.

In 1989 WACC held its first world congress in Manila, Philippines, on the theme "Communication for Community". The emphasis was placed on the need to defend democratic communication at world, national and local levels. In 1995, at WACC's second World Congress the main theme was "Communication for Human Dignity". Here the need was emphasized for communication to be understood as a social right and as one of the pillars for the exercise of world solidarity and for forming an international movement for a just and equitable order in social and communication policies.

Appendix 2

Communication for Human Dignity

The Mexico Declaration of the World Association for Christian Communication 7-11 October 1995

How can people of faith promote human dignity for all in a world where power structures, including the media, so often undermine it? This central question was the basis for reflection and recommendations of the 350 communicators from 85 countries who accepted the call of the World Association for Christian Communication to meet for a second World Congress in Metepec, Mexico, 7-11 October 1995. Participants noted the monumental changes which have taken place in the media and in the world since the first World Congress held in Manila in 1989. Recognizing the changes in the media environments since then — particularly the trends in monopolization of ownership, trivialization of contents and global spread — the Congress commits itself and calls upon all people of good will to respond to the demands of our time in the light of God's presence among us.

The Congress theme, "Communication for Human Dignity", arises from the understanding that all God's children are created in the image of God. All human beings, regardless of race, sex, age, religion, belief, class, physical or mental ability are endowed with the same dignity. The right to live in dignity is a universal principle from which spring all human rights. Whenever the dignity of a human being is violated, the dignity of life itself is jeopardized. Those who use and control the media must be made aware of this fundamental reality.

What we need today is information which leads to commitment, action, and transformation. In this spirit the Congress calls upon all people and especially communicators:

- to affirm the richness and power of communication within all cultures which are life-enhancing, particularly those of Indigenous People, learning from them, that we might stand together against dehumanizing forces;

- to challenge power structures within media, whether public or private, secular or religious, to incorporate values that enhance human dignity;
- to support the empowerment of women and men in all regions of the world who struggle for their dignity which is often denied by contemporary media;
- to interpret the potentials and limitations of new media, such as the Global Information Infrastructure, so that women and men are empowered to determine their own priorities and future.

To be human means to relate to others. Both the materially rich and poor are challenged by the claims of human dignity. Yet within the human community, dignity is most severely tested in relationship with the materially poor, powerless, and oppressed. The affirmation of their dignity is the basis for all struggles against dehumanization. Forces of economic structures, particularly some of those within the global free-market economy, stand in the way of this struggle. Only a deliberate and active solidarity with the weak and vulnerable can bring about change.

To be human is to communicate. Communication makes relationship possible. Through communication humanity can intensify its struggle against dehumanization so that the *oikoumene* — the whole inhabited world — may realize dignity and grace.

RECOMMENDATIONS

Communication ethics

People of faith working in communication ethics should strive to establish commonly acceptable, fundamental principles of ethics. These should be discussed and developed at the global, regional and local levels. Globally, these ethical principles must be made explicit in international negotiations. All communicators, public and private, should be encouraged vigorously to adopt as their central concern the values of diversity, community, identity, respect for all peoples, unconditional love, wholeness and truth. Regionally and locally, there is a need to build alliances with networks of grassroots organizations, communication trainers and programme makers to help shape, articulate and reflect the central ethical concerns of human dignity, the aspirations of communities, and the values of respect for life, truth and non-violence.

Economic issues

In our globalized free-market economy, increased privatization, so-called liberalization and de-regulation have resulted in media control by a handful of Western-based multinational corporations. Life qualities which cannot be quantified in financial terms are simply excluded from their calculations.

Christian communicators must press for the inclusion of these human values in every sphere available to them, seize every opportunity to utilize the new media creatively, develop viable alternative media wherever possible, organize to preserve and enhance the public sphere and media access rights of *all* people *everywhere*, and join with concerned colleagues in the creation of a more just new world economic order.

Human rights

Communicators must inform themselves about the instruments and mechanisms available in their countries to implement and protect human rights; disseminate human rights information to their respective audiences; and expose and denounce human rights abuses at all levels of government and private enterprises, and mobilize support for the victims of these abuses. Media workers should establish networks with human rights activists, locally, regionally and internationally, and support their activities in order to strengthen human rights lobbies, and participate in the formation and development of public education policies for the promotion of human rights.

Media education

The churches and non-governmental organizations should encourage people to use the media in innovative and responsible ways. The promotion of critically active audiences and responsible involvement in the formation of media policies should be among the main objectives of media education. Training in media literacy should be integrated into the various educational programmes at all levels, including churches, church and public schools and theological seminaries. Strategies in media education should take into account the specific media and cultural contexts in North and South.

Communication and religion

Christian churches and organizations should recognize and respond to the challenges of the media age and develop an organic rather than instrumental understanding of communication media. They should give attention to the reinterpretation of the contents of Christian discourse, as based on the deposit of faith. Christian communicators need to consider both the biblical text as well as cultural context in their communication work.

Christian communication

Christian communicators need to undertake serious theological reflection on their work and mission, particularly on the challenges posed by new information technologies. There should also be a strengthening of educational activities to meet these challenges. Christian communicators need to engage in a process of conscientization with respect to communication in pursuit of religious tolerance, justice and peace.

Social identity

Social identity and the sense of belonging are human necessities. They have either been attacked and suppressed, or extolled and idealized as ultimate reality, both resulting in tragic consequences. Social identities presuppose the right to use the mother tongue in all media of communication. The media should also encourage the creative use of symbols and images and other folk expressions by which people's identity is strengthened. In the movement of people from one society to another, new struggles for identities have emerged which embrace two or more cultural traditions. These diversities and new identities must also be recognized.

Ecology and environment

There is an urgent need to promote a theology of creation and thereby increase awareness about ecology and the environment. The insights and values of Indigenous People provide an important resource in environmental actions. Communication should be used to empower civil society and convince governments to deal with global ecological problems. In particular, media manipulation and censorship imposed by governments and the private sector about the nuclear industry, the testing of weapons and dumping practices should be exposed. Communicators should advocate for positive policies, laws and industrial codes of practice to protect the environment.

Indigenous perspectives

The concerns and contributions of Indigenous Peoples should be a priority for Christian communicators and for all concerned with a just communications order. This should be expressed in the full participation of Indigenous communicators in committees and planning groups, and in the implementation of programmes. Research and studies by and with Indigenous People on their world views and modes of communication should be given priority and publicized. Increased contacts with Indigenous Peoples should be encouraged, thereby sharing their concerns and aspirations.

Popular culture

Popular culture affirms deep-rooted human values, plural expressions as well as social contradictions. Popular culture is not a spectacle; rather, it is the creation and dissemination of meanings, experiences and values. There is a need to recognize the potential of popular culture to affirm and build human dignity, and resist exploitation.

Communicators have a responsibility to strengthen and bring together expressions of popular culture (e.g. religious rituals, oratory story-telling, songs and dance, jokes, theatre, games and riddles). In this way popular culture becomes an authentic expression of lived experience, rooted in reality as a means of developing human dignity.

Communication technology

There is an urgent need to understand more fully the implications of new communication technologies and to demystify the aura that surrounds them. Such analysis should include the diverse impact of technologies on the rights of peasants, the urban dispossessed, workers and societies in the two-thirds world.

Human communication is interactive, and technology should be a tool to aid that interactivity. It should not be used to exploit or to subordinate people. The new information technologies are, for example, dominated by the national languages of the major economic and political powers of the world. Special efforts need to be made to expose and redress the unequal access to information technologies. Voices for human dignity should be heard in the policy-making process of public and private entities that control technologies. At the international level, priority should be given to develop strategies to influence social and political structures in order to achieve more freedom, fairness and diversity in the media.

Gender issues

Gender issues in communication must be understood as pertaining to both sexes, and thus males must join with females in the struggle for a more just, equitable and balanced world information order. Women's absence from, and lack of power within existing communication structures cannot be changed by women working alone. Men must be their partners in this process. Women, together with men, should look through the prism of gender perspectives at the economic and political contexts of media control, media production, human rights and freedom of expression, media education and communication technologies.

There is a need to examine and critique prevailing definitions of power, masculinity and male-oriented value systems within communications structures. Training for women in new technologies, in the use of media for development, community media and in media production and management can be the means by which women are empowered. The resolutions of the women's conferences in Bangkok (1994) and Beijing (1995) should be propagated and implemented.